MOVIES

The World on Film

These and other books are included in the
Encyclopedia of Discovery and Invention
series:

Airplanes: The Lure of Flight
Atoms: Building Blocks of Matter
Clocks: Chronicling Time
Computers: Mechanical Minds
Genetics: Nature's Blueprints
Germs: Mysterious Microorganisms
Gravity: The Universal Force
Lasers: Humanity's Magic Light
Movies: The World on Film
Photography: Preserving the Past
Plate Tectonics: Earth's Shifting Crust
Printing Press: Ideas into Type
Radar: The Silent Detector
Railroads: Bridging the Continents
Telescopes: Searching the Heavens
Television: Electronic Pictures

MOVIES
The World on Film

by Deborah Hitzeroth
and Sharon Heerboth

The ENCYCLOPEDIA of
D·I·S·C·O·V·E·R·Y
and **INVENTION**

P.O. Box 289011, SAN DIEGO, CA 92198-0011

Library of Congress Cataloging-in-Publication Data

Hitzeroth, Deborah, 1961-
    Movies : the world on film / by Deborah Hitzeroth
and Sharon Heerboth.
        p.   cm. — (The Encyclopedia of discovery and
invention)
    Includes bibliographical references and index.
    Summary: A history of motion pictures, discussing such
aspects as their technological development, movie stars,
social aspects, censorship, and violence.
    ISBN 1-56006-210-X
    1. Motion pictures— Juvenile literature.   [1. Motion
pictures.]   I. Heerboth, Sharon, 1959-   II.   Title.
III. Series.
PN1994.5.H5   1991
791.43—dc20   91-16712

Contents

Foreword   7

Introduction   10

CHAPTER 1 ■ Illusions of Movement   12
   Moving pictures;
   Magic lanterns;
   The Zoetrope;
   Life in motion.

CHAPTER 2 ■ Pictures Come to Life   22
   Edison's moving pictures;
   The Kinetoscope;
   The Lumieres' Cinematographe;
   The first show;
   The Vitascope.

CHAPTER 3 ■ The Silent Screen   30
   Camera tricks;
   Theaters appear;
   The birth of Hollywood;
   Millionaire stars.

CHAPTER 4 ■ Pictures That Talk   40
   Sound accompanies film;
   Radio kills the silent film;
   The end of an era;
   Death of the silent film star;
   New fads.

CHAPTER 5 ■ The Golden Age to the Television Age   50
   Power of the studios;
   Lives under contract;
   The advent of television;
   Pictures with depth;
   Color and the big screen.

CHAPTER 6 ■ Movies and War 58
Pancho Villa's battles;
Supporting the war effort;
Movies go to war;
Portraying the horrors of war;
Antiwar movies.

CHAPTER 7 ■ Race, Censorship, and Ratings 70
Stirring hate;
Breaking barriers;
Censorship;
Forbidden topics;
The rating system.

CHAPTER 8 ■ Into the Future 84
Ride a magic carpet;
Touching new worlds;
Choose your own ending;
Movie magic.

Glossary 89
For Further Reading 90
Works Consulted 91
Index 92
About the Authors 95
Picture Credits 96

Foreword

The belief in progress has been one of the dominant forces in Western Civilization from the Scientific Revolution of the seventeenth century to the present. Embodied in the idea of progress is the conviction that each generation will be better off than the one that preceded it. Eventually, all peoples will benefit from and share in this better world. R.R. Palmer, in his *History of the Modern World,* calls this belief in progress "a kind of nonreligious faith that the conditions of human life" will continually improve as time goes on.

For over a thousand years prior to the seventeenth century, science had progressed little. Inquiry was largely discouraged, and experimentation, almost nonexistent. As a result, science became regressive and discovery was ignored. Benjamin Farrington, a historian of science, characterized it this way: "Science had failed to become a real force in the life of society. Instead there had arisen a conception of science as a cycle of liberal studies for a privileged minority. Science ceased to be a means of transforming the conditions of life." In short, had this intellectual climate continued, humanity's future would have been little more than a clone of its past.

Fortunately, these circumstances were not destined to last. By the seventeenth and eighteenth centuries, Western society was undergoing radical and favorable changes. And the changes that occurred gave rise to the notion that progress was a real force urging civilization forward. Surpluses of consumer goods were replacing substandard living conditions in most of Western Europe. Rigid class systems were giving way to social mobility. In nations like France and the United States, the lofty principles of democracy and popular sovereignty were being painted in broad, gilded strokes over the fading canvasses of monarchy and despotism.

But more significant than these social, economic, and political changes, the new age witnessed a rebirth of science. Centuries of scientific stagnation began crumbling before a spirit of scientific inquiry that spawned undreamed of technological advances. And it was the discoveries and inventions of scores of men and women that fueled these new technologies, dramatically increasing the ability of humankind to control nature—and, many believed, eventually to guide it.

It is a truism of science and technology that the results derived from observation and experimentation are not finalities. They are part of a process. Each discovery is but one piece in a continuum bridging past and present and heralding an extraordinary future. The heroic age of the Scientific Revolution was simply a start. It laid a foundation upon which succeeding generations of imaginative thinkers could build. It kindled the belief that progress is possible as long as there were gifted men and women who would respond to society's needs. When Antonie van Leeuwenhoek observed *Animalcules* (little animals) through his high-powered microscope in 1683, the discovery did not end there. Others followed who would call these "little animals" bacteria and, in time, recognize their role in the process of health and disease. Robert Koch, a German bacteriologist and winner of the Nobel Prize in Physiology and Medicine, was one of these men. Koch firmly established that bacteria are responsible for causing infectious diseases. He identified, among others, the causative organisms of anthrax and tuberculosis. Alexander Fleming, another Nobel Laureate, progressed still further in the quest to understand and control bacteria. In 1928, Fleming discovered penicillin, the antibiotic wonder drug. Penicillin, and the generations of antibiotics that succeeded it, have done more to

prevent premature death than any other discovery in the history of humankind. And as civilization hastens toward the twenty-first century, most agree that the conquest of van Leeuwenhoek's "little animals" will continue.

The *Encyclopedia of Discovery and Invention* examines those discoveries and inventions that have had a sweeping impact on life and thought in the modern world. Each book explores the ideas that led to the invention or discovery, and, more importantly, how the world changed and continues to change because of it. The series also highlights the people behind the achievements—the unique men and women whose singular genius and rich imagination have altered the lives of everyone. Enhanced by photographs and clearly explained technical drawings, these books are comprehensive examinations of the building blocks of human progress.

MOVIES

The World on Film

MOVIES

Introduction

On any given night, thousands of people around the world will go to the movies. In spite of home video, Nintendo, and cable television, nothing seems to replace the cushy seats, big screen, and buttered popcorn of the crowded movie theater.

Movies are such a part of our lives that most people can name a favorite scene, dialogue, actor, or actress from a movie. For many, a movie has stirred deep emotions, including sorrow, empathy, hatred, fear, and happiness. In this way, movies rank among the other influential art forms such as painting,

photography, and plays. In fact, movies can be used to combine or highlight many of these other forms of art. A movie can record pure visual sensation much like a photograph or a painting. Movies can reenact a play and preserve and immortalize the performance on the screen. Some movies combine art forms in new ways. And even when movies are pure entertainment, telling an unfolding story on the screen, they are preserved in our memories just as other forms of art can be.

It is easy to forget the influence movies have on our memories and on our collective understanding of the world. Our images of gangsters, adventurers, murderers, and even characters

■ ■ ■ TIMELINE: MOVIES

1 ▷   2 ▷   3 ▷   4 ▷ 5 ▷   6 ▷ 7 ▷

1 ■ 1600s
First magic lanterns, the earliest form of projectors, are invented.

2 ■ 1822
Louis Jacques Mande Daguerre invents the diorama.

3 ■ 1834
William George Horner invents the Zoetrope.

4 ■ 1887
Hannibal Williston Goodwin invents film. George Eastman buys the invention and begins to mass-produce it.

5 ■ 1889
Thomas Edison introduces the Kinetograph, the first true motion picture camera.

6 ■ 1894
Edison unveils the Kinetoscope, a device that lets one person at a time view motion pictures.

7 ■ 1895
Auguste and Louis Lumiere give the first public showing of the Cinematographe. This device projects motion pictures on a screen.

in books are largely drawn from movies. We would recognize and feel we know characters such as Indiana Jones and Luke Skywalker. In addition to these images, movies affect our opinions about violence, sex, racism, and other social concerns portrayed on the screen. Movies such as *The Silence of the Lambs* (1991), with its explicit murder scenes, *Batman* (1989), with its disturbing violence, and *Blue Velvet* (1986), with its mixture of sex and violence, make us wonder how far movies should be allowed to go in their portrayal of these controversial topics. People worry that these images might cause others to reenact them in real life. Parents wonder if they should shelter their children for fear these images may haunt their imaginations long after the movie ends. In short, society views movies as powerful for the visual record they leave on our psyches, our imaginations, and on our mores.

Interestingly, it is the purpose of movies—to entertain—that seems to disguise their importance to society. Somehow, the tales of wonder, horror, and humor that movies spin almost lead us to forget their influence on our ideas. That, perhaps, is why movies, like books, paintings, and photographs, are in no danger of disappearing even as technology advances. They continue to inspire, entertain, and keep us spellbound in the dark.

---

8 > 9 > 10 > 11 > 12 > 13 > 14 > 15

8 ■ 1903
Edwin S. Porter produces *The Great Train Robbery,* the first narrative film.

9 ■ 1905
First nickelodeon opens in Pittsburgh, Pennsylvania.

10 ■ 1917
Technicolor is introduced.

11 ■ 1922
The Motion Picture Producers and Distributors Association hires Will Hays to regulate the content of films.

12 ■ 1927
Al Jolson sings and talks in *The Jazz Singer.*

13 ■ 1950
Television overtakes movies in popularity; color replaces black-and-white movies.

14 ■ 1984
Rating system is changed to include the new classification of PG-13.

15 ■ 1990
Rating system drops the X classification and replaces it with NC-17 (no children under 17 allowed).

Illusions of Movement

In the United States and Europe during the 1800s, exciting technological developments and new discoveries were being made daily. Amazing new inventions captured public attention. Automobiles began to appear on the roads, and for the first time ever, people listened to recorded music at home, thanks to an invention called the phonograph. People were equally fascinated by the telegraph, a new device that could send messages over great distances. And scientists in Great Britain and Italy were laying the groundwork for the invention of the radio.

To compete with these marvels of science, performers and artists began

In the 1800s, people were fascinated by new inventions such as the phonograph.

searching for ways to make their productions more exciting to the public. Some painters began painting bigger-than-life scenes on the walls of exhibit halls. These panoramic murals usually depicted action scenes that were divided into segments. Dramatic battles and ships at sea were popular topics. When viewed together and illuminated in sequence, the segments blended to create the illusion of moving pictures.

A Scottish painter named Robert Barker was famous for using this technique. Barker surrounded spectators with huge panoramas, cleverly lit to enhance the reality of his work. People throughout Europe were enthusiastic about the panorama shows. Many depicted historic battles, such as the Battle of Waterloo, in which the French general Napoleon Bonaparte was defeated near Brussels, Belgium, in 1815.

Another artist, Louis Jacques Mande Daguerre of France, improved on Barker's panoramas by painting the scenes on translucent fabric screens instead of walls. By using this fabric, Daguerre was able to shine light through his paintings to highlight certain scenes.

Moving Pictures

Daguerre used these lighted paintings to create a new type of presentation called a diorama. To view a diorama, the audience sat in a darkened theater, surrounded on all sides by the painted

The telegraph, one of the greatest technological inventions of the 1880s, allowed people to send messages over long distances.

screens. Daguerre lighted and dimmed the lamps behind different areas of the scene to tell a story. Before the diorama, audiences attended theaters to watch actors perform in plays. The diorama marked the first time audiences attended theaters to watch painted pictures that seemed to move.

If the diorama were telling the story of a war, for example, lights might shine briefly behind a scene of charging soldiers with weapons held high. The soldiers would disappear into the dark when the lights behind the panel were turned off. Meanwhile, lights on another side of the theater would illuminate pictures of the opposing warriors. Although they gave the appearance of movement, the pictures did not actually move. The dioramas were important for another reason, however. In creating dioramas, Daguerre was the first person to manipulate lights and pictures to tell

stories, both key elements of what one day would be known as motion pictures.

Daguerre opened his first diorama theater in 1822 in London. The theater consisted of two picture rooms where diorama scenes were displayed and an area for audience seating. The diorama scenes were stationary, but the theater was designed so that the seats could be turned from one scene to the other. Moving the audience helped promote the illusion that the diorama pictures were moving. Audiences were amazed by pictures that seemed to jump out of the darkness at them, and crowds rushed to the theaters to see them.

Magic Lanterns

Despite their popularity, dioramas were soon overshadowed by another light-and-picture show produced by a device called a magic lantern. Magic lanterns seemed to magically produce pictures in a darkened room, but there was nothing supernatural about them. Magic lanterns produced images by using a simple process called projection. Projection is the effect of placing a brightly lit object in front of a magnifying lens. This produces an image that can be displayed on a flat surface, like a screen, a long distance away from the lens.

Magic lanterns got their name from early versions built in the 1600s that looked like lanterns. Actually, the nineteenth-century magic lanterns were ordinary rectangular boxes with a round hole cut in one side. A magnifying lens similar to a magnifying glass covered the hole. The lantern operator slid transparent pictures mounted on glass behind the lens. To make the magic lantern display images, a lighted candle was placed inside the box. The light from the candle flame projected the picture through the lens and onto the wall of a darkened room. The image could be made larger by moving the lantern away from the wall or smaller by moving it closer to the wall. These early projectors were very popular. Traveling showpeople took them from town to town throughout Europe to display their magic powers.

Into the Limelight

Magic lanterns remained popular in Europe for two hundred years, especially in France, Germany, and Great Britain. By

French artist Louis Jacques Mande Daguerre invented the diorama.

This nineteenth-century engraving shows a man peering into a Praxinoscope, or "motion-scope," while a child looks on. The Praxinoscope, invented by Emile Reynaud of France, was the first machine to fully project moving pictures.

the late 1800s, the British had perfected the art of making magic lanterns. These lanterns were much more powerful than the earlier ones. They were illuminated by limelights, which burned lime to create a bright, white light. The limelights produced a brilliant beam that could project images across a large auditorium. Some theaters were equipped with three or four lanterns that could be used for special effects. By using multiple lanterns, projectionists were able to make one scene disappear gradually while another slowly appeared in its place.

Some lanterns were also equipped with gears to move the lamp closer to and farther from the screen while automatically retaining the picture's focus.

By manipulating the controls, projectionists could position the lantern so that villains loomed huge on the screen as their helpless victims cowered beneath them. This innovation was created by inventor Etienne Gaspard Robertson of Belgium. Robertson called his new system of projection the Phantasmagoria because he used it to produce ghostly images and phantoms. Pictures and reports of Robertson's audiences show men recoiling from the projected ghosts and women fainting in fear.

The success of the Phantasmagoria created a large audience for projected pictures. Inventors soon added devices to Robertson's machine that made his phantoms seem even more lifelike.

Henry Langdon Childe, a British

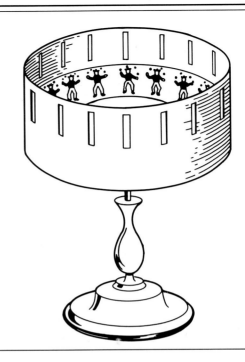
projectionist, developed a way of projecting one image on top of another. Childe created this effect by using two projectors. By closing the lens of one projector and then slowly opening the lens of the other, he could cause one image to fade into the other. This double image made it appear as though one image magically changed into the other. The pictures seemed to be moving, but this illusion did not satisfy everyone. Some artists and inventors wanted more than just the appearance of motion. They wanted to create pictures that really moved. For this, inventors turned to a simple child's toy for inspiration.

Child's Play

In 1834, British inventor William George Horner began selling a toy called the Zoetrope, or the "wheel of life." The Zoetrope consisted of a small metal drum with pictures drawn on the inside. Each picture showed part of a series of actions. The first drawing, for example, might be of a juggler throwing a ball in the air. The second drawing would show the ball flying over the juggler's head, and the third would be a view of the juggler catching the ball. The Zoetrope drum had slits cut in the sides for the user to look through. When the drum was turned rapidly on its center post, the individual still pictures seemed to form one moving picture.

This effect is called persistence of vision. It occurs because the retina of the eye retains an image for a fraction of a second after the image has disappeared. This means that when a succession of still pictures is changed rapidly, the human eye merges one picture into another and sees the illusion of movement. This is the principle on which the Zoetrope and, eventually, motion pictures were based. The Zoetrope fascinated children in Europe. But its real importance was in how it inspired other inventors. In 1876, Emile Reynaud of France built an improved version of the Zoetrope, designed for adult entertainment. Reynaud's invention was the first device to project moving pictures.

Reynaud first removed the viewing slits from the toy and replaced them with mirrors along the center post inside the toy's drum. These mirrors reflected a brighter and clearer picture than the Zoetrope's viewing slots. Next, Reynaud borrowed some of the mechanics of the magic lantern. He drew pictures on paper and then applied wax to the paper to make it translucent. He placed a bright light behind the pictures so that the light would shine through them and onto the mirrors. After the image struck the mirrors, it was re-

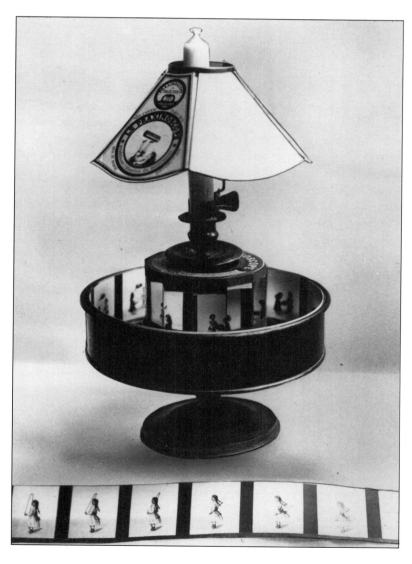

This photograph, made in 1887, shows a Praxinoscope projector and, at the bottom, a projection image of a girl skipping rope.

In 1873, wanting to prove that, at a certain point, a running horse had all four hooves off the ground, the governor of California hired photographer Eadweard Muybridge to photograph the governor's racehorse. Muybridge mounted twenty-four cameras along the edge of a track and placed trip wires over the track to trigger the cameras. As the horse galloped past, it tripped the cameras. Two photos showed the horse with all four hooves off the ground.

flected through a magnifying lens and projected onto a screen. Reynaud called his invention the Praxinoscope, which meant "motion-scope."

The Praxinoscope was the first machine that seemed to project fully moving pictures, which looked much like modern animated cartoons. Reynaud's skits showed animated figures fighting, juggling, or jumping through hoops. Audiences loved his drawings, which seemed to dance across the screen by themselves.

Although popular with the public, Reynaud's machine was not very practical. Reynaud drew each picture by hand, which meant it took hours to create a single short set of images. Inventors needed a way to produce pictures quickly. They found their answer in photography, which also opened the way for true motion pictures.

Photography is the process of capturing an image on a light-sensitive surface. The development of photography made it possible to capture and reproduce images of real life. Without photography, motion pictures would not have evolved past the point of animated cartoons.

The person who made this possible was a British photographer named Henry Fox Talbot. In 1871, Talbot developed a method of taking pictures very rapidly, which enabled photographers to take pictures of movement. Before Talbot, film had to be exposed for up to fifteen minutes to record an image. This type of film was useless for motion pictures because if the subject moved, the picture would be blurred. But Talbot developed a film that needed an exposure time of only one-hundredth of a second to record an image. This fast exposure time was essential for recording action. With the new film, photographers could capture people in the process of dancing or running and could get a clear picture of anything that was moving at the time of the photograph.

Capturing Life in Motion

Talbot's fast photography caught the interest of Eadweard Muybridge, a young photographer from England who moved to the United States to pursue his career. In 1873, Muybridge was hired by

California governor Leland Stanford to photograph his prized racehorse. Stanford had made a bet of twenty-five thousand dollars with his friends that at a certain point, a running horse had all four feet off the ground. The horse's movement was too rapid for the human eye to follow, so Stanford turned to photography to catch the motion and win his bet.

Muybridge's Solution

Muybridge was faced with quite a challenge. Photography was fast enough to capture the image, but cameras were equipped to take only one picture at a time. Muybridge spent two years experimenting with different ways to obtain the type of photos the governor wanted. Finally, Muybridge found a solution. He mounted twenty-four cameras on posts one foot apart and ran wires across the race track. As the horse ran past the cameras, he broke the wires and tripped the switches on the cameras. The photographs clearly showed the horse in each stage of its stride, and two pictures showed the horse with all four feet off the ground. These photos won the governor's bet. But more important, they proved that photographs could capture life in motion.

Muybridge proved that a series of photographs taken quickly one after another could capture all of the elements of movement. When his photographs were viewed rapidly, they made it seem as though the horse were actually running. This series of still photographs was the basis for motion pictures.

Muybridge continued to photograph animals in motion. To further his studies of movement, he devised a way to project movement using a series of photographs taken in rapid succession. He traced the photographs onto glass slides and mounted them on a rotating wheel. With the help of a magic lantern to project the images rapidly one after another onto a screen, the animals seemed to come alive. In 1882, *Scientific American* magazine wrote that Muybridge's device "threw upon the screen . . . the living, moving animals. Nothing was wanting but the clatter of hoofs upon the turf."

Muybridge's device was called a Zoopraxiscope, which meant "animal-habit scope." It was much like the Praxinoscope. The major difference between the two instruments was the type of pictures they projected. The Praxinoscope projected hand-drawn cartoons, and Muybridge's machine projected photographs. The Zoopraxiscope was the first to use images taken from real life and to create the illusion of movement. The Zoopraxiscope was very popular. Audiences were amazed by the machine's capability of displaying motion on a screen. Muybridge spent several years touring the United States and Europe showing pictures with his Zoopraxiscope.

The Photo Revolver

At the same time that Muybridge was touring Europe, a French physiologist named Etienne-Jules Marey was also studying animal movement. Marey was particularly interested in the flight of birds. He used a machine invented by French astronomer Pierre Jules Janssen to help him view birds in flight. Janssen's device, called a "photographic revolver," allowed a photographer to

capture a number of images very quickly. Janssen had used the camera to study the movement of the planet Venus. The camera consisted of a lens, two revolving disks, and a timing device. A slitted disk was positioned on top of a single round photographic plate. The device was run by a clock that rotated the bottom disk every seventy-two seconds, allowing Janssen to record forty-eight successive images of Venus on a single plate.

Using this idea, Marey built a similar device on a much smaller scale. Marey called his camera a *fusil photographique*, or "photo gun." It was the first portable camera capable of live-action photography. His device resembled a short rifle, with the bullet chamber replaced by a photographic disk. The action was much like that of a machine gun. When the operator pulled the trigger, the shutter opened. This exposed one section of the disk before the shutter closed and the disk rotated to the next position. This action was repeated until the disk was

In this nineteenth-century engraving (top), French physiologist Etienne-Jules Marey fires his "photo gun," the first portable camera to take live-action photos. Marey (bottom) continued redesigning the gun, until it took 120 pictures per second.

back to its starting position. In this fashion, Marey was able to take twelve pictures in one second.

Marey continued to improve his photo gun until he could take up to 120 pictures per second. These pictures often overlapped each other and blurred because Marey had no way of holding his photographic paper steady. Imperfect though it was, the photo gun was the first device able to rapidly record a number of successive movements. This allowed Marey to capture an entire movement while it was being performed. Because of this development, Marey's camera was a great improvement over Muybridge's method.

When shown in sequence, Marey's pictures gave an audience the illusion of watching motion pictures. Because he was able to capture the entire movement, Marey's projected pictures were more lifelike than Muybridge's. Marey's camera was a great advancement in the development of a true motion picture camera.

Pictures Come to Life

The development of motion pictures came about with the help of a minister and a billiard ball. Traditionally, billiard balls were made of ivory, but in the 1800s ivory became too expensive. Companies began looking for an inexpensive substitute. While doing research for one company in 1868, inventor John Wesley Hyatt came up with a new material he named Celluloid. It was made of nitrocellulose, camphor, and alcohol.

Celluloid was strong and stiff, and when it was made into thin strips, it was transparent. This meant light could be shown through it. This substance quickly became popular with photographers and magic lantern projectionists. Celluloid was a great improvement over glass and waxed paper because it was more flexible than glass and more transparent than waxed paper. But it still had problems. Celluloid was too stiff to be used for long magic lantern shows. It tended to crack and break when it was used in strips that were longer than fifty feet. This meant that a typical magic lantern show would last only a minute before the Celluloid broke.

The brittle nature of Celluloid bothered Hannibal Williston Goodwin, a minister who often entertained his congregation with magic lantern shows. Goodwin changed the mix of chemicals that made up Celluloid and created a new material that he called Photographic Pellicle, or film.

Film had one distinct advantage over Celluloid. It was flexible. Film

One man's work to find an inexpensive material for making billiard balls resulted in the creation of celluloid. This in turn led to the invention of photographic film.

could be used in long strips without cracking or breaking. This meant Goodwin could present a continuous show, sometimes lasting as long as three minutes, with his magic lantern projector. And Goodwin was not the only person who was eager to put the new, flexible film to use.

American industrialist George Eastman saw promise in it, too, and bought the rights to mass-produce Goodwin's film. Eastman had been working on ways to broaden the appeal of cameras, which were still viewed mostly as tools for professionals. Easy-to-use film would help make the camera more popular, Eastman thought.

Edison's Moving Pictures

To American inventor Thomas Edison, the new film seemed a perfect choice for bringing motion pictures to the public. Edison was not interested in motion pictures for art, science, or even entertainment, but he wanted a device to help sell his earlier invention, the phonograph. Edison envisioned his phonograph being used to record testimony in courtrooms across the nation. At the same time, Edison thought, a motion picture camera would provide moving pictures of the court proceedings.

Edison's first motion picture devices

Shown here in the 1880s, American inventor Thomas Edison wanted to use motion pictures to help sell his earlier invention, the phonograph.

were the Kinetograph, a camera, and the Kinetoscope, a projector. Though they were called Edison inventions,

Here, long strips of modern motion picture film are being developed, or processed. In the early days of film, when celluloid strips were longer than fifty feet, they tended to crack and break.

most of the work was done by his assistant, William Laurie Kennedy Dickson.

The Kinetograph, completed in 1889, had two important parts. The first was a stop-motion device that held the film in a fixed position while it was exposed. The second important part consisted of perforated film strips, held in place by reels and spools. Together, these innovations plus a system for moving the film past the shutter, frame by frame at a fixed speed, kept the image on the film from being blurred.

The Kinetograph was the best moving picture camera available, but it still had problems. The Kinetograph was a huge camera. It was bigger than a piano and weighed more than one ton. Because of its size, and because it needed electricity to run, the Kinetograph was not portable. For this reason, Dickson built a special studio in which to make films with the Kinetograph. The studio was a tar-papered hut with a roof that could be rolled back to let the sun in. The room was built to revolve on a pivot so that it could receive the most amount of sun. At one end of the room, where the sunlight was the brightest, was a stage. At the other end was the massive Kinetograph. At first, Dickson and Edison started the film rolling and filmed anything that moved. Nothing was wasted, including footage of a worker sneezing. Edison called that film *Fred Ott's Sneeze.* Later, Edison invited circus performers and touring acts to perform on his filming stage. Buffalo Bill Cody, Sandow the Strongman, "Little Sure Shot" Annie Oakley, and the dancer Carmencita were some of Edison's first film stars.

A Creative Difference

Edison and Dickson disagreed about the type of projector they would need for these moving pictures. Dickson wanted a machine that would project moving images on a screen for large audiences. Edison thought that Dickson's idea would bankrupt the company. He claimed that if his pictures were shown to large audiences, too few projectors would be needed. Edison finally persuaded Dickson to abandon the idea of a large projection machine, and Dickson went to work building a device that only one person at a time could use. The result was the Kinetoscope.

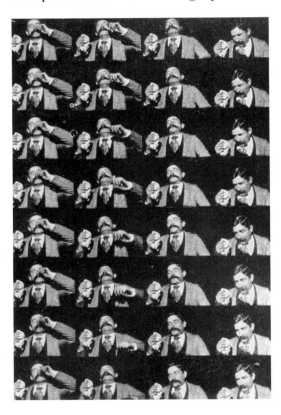

When Thomas Edison operated his Kinetograph camera, he photographed anything that moved, including a worker sneezing. Fred Ott's Sneeze, *recorded in 1893, became the world's first motion picture close-up sequence.*

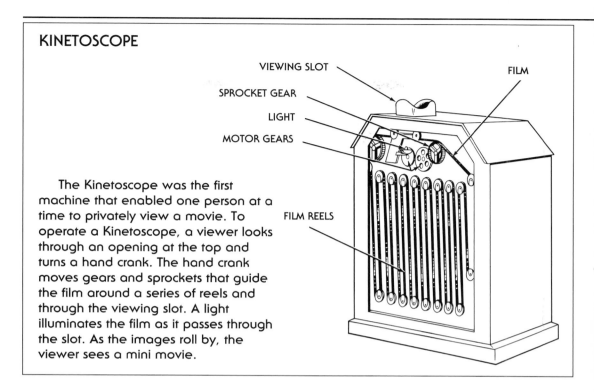

KINETOSCOPE

VIEWING SLOT

FILM

SPROCKET GEAR

LIGHT

MOTOR GEARS

FILM REELS

The Kinetoscope was the first machine that enabled one person at a time to privately view a movie. To operate a Kinetoscope, a viewer looks through an opening at the top and turns a hand crank. The hand crank moves gears and sprockets that guide the film around a series of reels and through the viewing slot. A light illuminates the film as it passes through the slot. As the images roll by, the viewer sees a mini movie.

The Kinetoscope was unveiled in 1894 in New York. It held a fifty-foot loop of film that ran continuously in front of a light. Because the films jumped and flickered, they were soon called "flickers." The Kinetoscope was designed to allow one person to "peep in" at the pictures. The peep show customer stepped up to a tall box, dropped a penny in a slot, and turned the hand crank on the side. A shutter slid open over a glass-covered keyhole, and the viewer was treated to a private movie. These movies lasted about thirty seconds each.

Despite their poor quality and simplistic presentations, the new moving pictures fascinated the public. Kinetoscope parlors sprang up all over the United States, and Edison had a hard time meeting the demand for his machines. Even with the popularity of his

Kinetoscope, Edison thought the public interest in motion pictures was a passing fad. Dickson could not persuade him to continue refining his cameras and films or to build a bigger, better projector. Edison was so sure that there was no future in motion pictures that he refused to spend the additional $150 to register his patents abroad. Those who hold a patent have the exclusive right to manufacture or sell an invention. Edison would soon regret his decision.

Copycats

A medical instrument maker named Robert Paul discovered that Edison had failed to register his patent on the Kinetoscope in Great Britain. Paul quickly copied the machine and began marketing it in Europe. At first, Paul did not produce his own movies. Instead, he bought movies from Edison's company. Edison could not stop Paul from copying his machine, but he eventually did refuse to sell movies to anyone using the copied machine. This only encouraged Paul and others to build their own cameras and make their own films. These films showed foreign locations that many Americans had never seen. Soon Kinetoscope exhibitors were buying more of the foreign-made films than Edison's. But the worst blow to Edison was yet to come.

In France, Auguste and Louis Lumiere bought a copied projector from Paul. By 1895, they had perfected their own version of the Kinetoscope. The Lumiere brothers had designed a combination camera and projector. They called their invention the Cinematographe. The camera part of the Cinematographe was based on the same principle as Edison's Kinetograph, with a few important changes. Like Edison, the Lumieres used perforated film in their machine. Edison used the perforations and a mechanism to advance and hold the film steady in the camera. The Lumieres extended this idea to the projector so that a claw mechanism moved the film forward, frame by frame, and held it in place in both the camera and projector. This mechanism was called a stop-motion device. By using the same mechanism to move and pause the film in both camera and projector, the Lumieres eliminated much of the flicker that plagued the Kinetoscope.

The other important difference in the Lumieres' machine was its size. Edison designed the Kinetoscope to use an electric motor, making it too large and heavy to move from its specially constructed studio. The Lumieres used a hand crank to turn the rolls of film and a lantern to provide light. Thus, the Cinematographe was much smaller, lightweight, and portable. It weighed only about sixteen pounds, which meant the Lumieres could take their machine out of the studio and all over the world to make their films.

The First Show

The Lumiere brothers made several films and then approached the owners of the most popular theaters in Paris with their plan of showing movies to large audiences. None were interested. The theater owners doubted the films would bring in enough people to pay even for the room rental. Finally, in frustration, the Lumieres rented a small

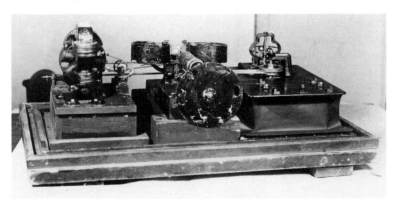

This 1889 photograph shows Thomas Edison and William Laurie Kennedy Dickson's motion picture camera, the Kinetograph. Although simplistic and crude, this machine recorded movie images much like today's elaborate cameras do.

basement called the Salon Indien, located under a popular dinner theater named the Grand Cafe. The owner of the Grand Cafe had so little faith in the public's desire to see these moving pictures that he charged the brothers a flat rental rate instead of the normal rate of 20 percent of the admissions.

The first showing was December 28, 1895. None of the journalists or art patrons the Lumieres had invited came. Local papers ignored the opening altogether. Only thirty-five people were on hand to see the very first motion pictures shown to the public. But word of the films spread quickly. Less than three weeks later, more than two thousand people a day were crowding into the Salon Indien.

The films that people were standing in line to see were very simple scenes from everyday life. Each strip of film

This nineteenth-century illustration shows the interior of a Kinetographic theater in New York City. Boxers spar under the bright lights while another man operates the Kinetograph camera.

was about fifty feet long and ran for about one minute. The titles shown included *Lunch Hour at the Lumiere Factory, Arrival of a Train at the Station, Baby's Breakfast,* and *A Bathing Beach.* The au-

LUMIERES' MOVIE CAMERA WITH CLAW FOR STOP MOTION

The Lumiere brothers developed a combination camera and projector that used special film to eliminate the bouncing and annoying "flickering" that characterized early movies. A small claw pulls a strip of perforated film one frame at a time past the shutter of the camera. When the shutter opens, the claw has secured the frame of film in front of the lens so that it can be projected onto the screen. When the shutter closes, the claw pulls the strip down one more frame. This cycle is repeated twenty-four times per second. People watching the film see continuous motion without flickering.

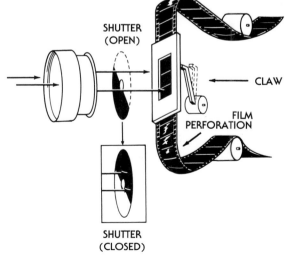

dience was amazed by the lifelike movement of the trees in the background scenery. The realism of the train roaring across the screen frightened many viewers, and several people in the front rows ran to escape the waves from the bathing beach.

These early films did not tell a story and were completely unedited. Yet audiences were delighted, not with the contents of the film but with the movement. Many people saw each film six or seven times. The nature scenes were the most intriguing to viewers, who were fascinated by the way leaves moved in the wind and waves broke on the shore.

The Lumieres capitalized on the public's enchantment with the short films and sent their cameramen all over Europe to film newsworthy events and local scenery. Because the Cinematographe was portable, the Lumieres were able to film some of the most important events of their time, including the 1901 funeral of Queen Victoria of England.

Back to the United States

The Lumieres expanded their moviemaking business throughout Europe. They sent representatives to the United States to make new films and to exhibit the Cinematographe. Before opening their exhibit in a new town, they would film scenes of the town and townspeople and then add these scenes to their films. People were thrilled at the sight of their own town and friends projected on the screen. These films were life-size, something the American public had never seen. They flocked to the new films, and the Cinematographe quickly became more popular than Edison's Kinetoscope.

Despite the popularity of the Cinematographe, the Lumieres believed moving picture shows were only a novelty and that the public would soon lose interest in the films. So they decided to make as much money as they could from selling their films before public interest died.

Like the Lumieres, Edison was also sure that people's fascination with movies would not last. When he abandoned further experiments to improve the Kinetoscope, Dickson left the company. Dickson and two other former Edison employees, Hermann Casler and Henry Marvin, formed a new company called American Mutoscope and Biograph Company, better known as Biograph.

Using Dickson's designs, they built their own cameras and full-size projectors. The machines were better than Edison's. Biograph's projector was called the Mutoscope. The motion pictures shown on the Mutoscope were steadier, clearer, and almost seven times larger than any others at the time. In November 1896, the Mutoscope was exhibited at Hammerstein's Music Hall in New York City. It became so popular after just one showing that the newly formed company could not fill all its orders.

Edison could not ignore the popularity of motion pictures any longer. People were bypassing his Kinetoscopes in favor of the rival company's life-size moving pictures. Edison was far from perfecting a similar projector, so he decided to purchase a newly designed projector from another young American inventor, Thomas Armat. Edison agreed to give Armat credit for the design but wanted to market the projector under his own name. Armat agreed, and the public was soon invited to see "Edison's latest marvel—the Vitascope."

The Vitascope was an electrically powered projector with a stop-motion device like the one used by the Lumieres. Armat's machine also included the latest innovation, the Latham Loop. Invented by camera builders Gray and Otway Latham, the loop was a major improvement in projector design. Two more sprockets were added in the pro-

Thomas Edison (above) was credited with inventing the Kinetograph, a camera, and the Kinetoscope, a projector. However, much of the work was done by his assistant, William Laurie Kennedy Dickson.

jector, one above and one below the lens. The film was looped over these sprockets to reduce the stress on the film as it was pulled from reel to reel. This kept long pieces of the film from breaking. Without this invention, films over 150 feet, or about three minutes, would not have been possible. Long rolls were very heavy, and the weight of the roll put so much tension on the film as it was being pulled through the projector, that it often snapped. The Latham Loop reduced the tension placed on the film and solved this problem.

Losing Interest

Kinetoscopes soon disappeared as the public turned to the Cinematographe, the Mutascope, and the Vitascope for entertainment. The Edison, Biograph, and Vitagraph film companies set up factories to meet the demand for new films. They turned out hundreds of films as quickly and cheaply as possible. The filmmakers were not concerned with what they filmed, as long as it moved. The films had no story or plot, and many were just scenes of trees waving in the wind or waves crashing on the shore. All of the early film companies copied each other's most popular films, then renamed and resold them. The films soon became boring and repetitious, and the public began to lose interest.

The Silent Screen

French magician and puppeteer George Melies brought silent storytelling to motion pictures. Melies saw one of the Lumieres' first shows and was so taken with the moving pictures that he offered to buy the Cinematographe before the show was even over. Auguste Lumiere replied, "Young man, you should be grateful, since although my invention is not for sale, it would undoubtedly ruin you. It can be exploited for a certain time as a scientific curiosity but, apart from that, it has no commercial future whatsoever."

Melies was not discouraged. He soon bought a projector from English inventor Robert Paul. Melies took apart the projector, studied its mechanisms, and built a camera that would work along with it. He began producing his own films to be shown in the Theatre Robert-Houdin in Paris. His films were no different from those sold by the Lumieres and Edison, until Melies stumbled upon trick photography. Melies's trick photography helped spark the public's interest in motion pictures again during a time when people were becoming bored with the kind of movies made by Edison and the Lumieres.

Camera Tricks

Melies's discovery happened by accident one afternoon as he was filming a scene of a typical Paris street. The film got stuck in the camera, and Melies had to stop filming to fix it. After rewinding the film, he continued until the end of the reel. When he later developed and ran the film, Melies discovered a curious effect. In one scene, a bus driving down the street mysteriously transformed into a hearse. Melies examined the film to see what had happened. In studying the film, he realized he had rewound it too far after freeing the jammed film. When he continued filming, he used film that had already been exposed. This caused one scene to fade into another, making it look like one object was actually becoming something else. Melies decided to use this and

This 1902 painting by French filmmaker George Melies depicts a scene from one of Melies's most famous films, A Trip to the Moon. *Melies was a master of film illusion.*

This 1902 photograph shows the New York headquarters of George Melies's Star Film Company. Even after the success of films like A Trip to the Moon, Cinderella, *and* Red Riding Hood, *Melies died as a pauper in Paris.*

other photographic tricks in his films. He used stop-action photography to make objects disappear, then reappear in another spot. He did this by exposing one frame of the film, stopping the film, moving the objects being photographed, then exposing the next frame. By doing this over and over, Melies could make chairs dance, people disappear, or an elephant turn into a mouse.

Magician and showman that he was, Melies became known as the master of film illusion. He started his own moviemaking business called Star Film Company, and he made hundreds of fantasy films. Melies built a fifty-five-by-twenty-foot, glass-enclosed studio in Paris so he could use the outdoors as scenery for his films. Melies's films were beautiful, lavish productions with elaborate costumes and decorations. In *A Trip to the Moon*, for example, Melies used fantastic outer space costumes and a rocket ship. His most popular films were science fiction stories like *The Impossible Voyage* and fairy tales like *Cinderella* and *Red Riding Hood.* These were the first movies to tell

a story, and audiences loved them. In *Cinderella*, the actors wore beautiful costumes and walked in regal settings. With the help of his camera tricks, Melies turned mice into horses and a pumpkin into a royal coach and made a fairy godmother appear out of thin air. At that time, it was a magical sight. *Cinderella* was a long film, running more than four minutes, but audiences stayed to watch it over and over again.

The Novelty Wears Off

While other film companies were still distributing one- or two-minute films of workers leaving a factory or trains arriving at a station, Melies was thrilling his audiences with fantastic stories. The public flocked to see his latest films but were turning their backs and closing their coin purses on the other filmmakers. By 1902, Star Film Company was the largest film producer in the world.

After a while, other film distributors started copying Melies's and each other's films. Some even took Melies's films, re-named them, and sold them as their own work. This resulted in a lot of films but very little variety. Soon, the public even tired of Melies's films and stopped coming to see the newest offerings.

The novelty had worn off. Films lost their place in the spotlight. They moved to variety houses where they shared the stage with magicians, dancers, and vaudeville performers. They became so unpopular that they were used as "chasers" at the end of vaudeville acts to discourage people from sitting through the show twice. It seemed that Edison was right about his prediction that there was no future in motion pictures.

Master of the Shot

In 1902, a projectionist turned director named Edwin S. Porter decided to try something different. Porter worked for the Edison company and had watched films rise and fall in popularity. He be-lieved that the reason people stopped watching motion pictures was because they were bored. Most filmmakers just turned their cameras on and filmed whatever passed in front of the lens. Even those who told simple stories used the camera as though it were a specta-tor at a play. The camera never moved from a fixed position, and performers entered and exited the film as though on a stage. All of the action was filmed and shown in the sequence in which it occurred on-screen. Films were realistic, but they lacked drama and suspense.

Porter thought it would be better to show the film in the sequence that made the story most exciting. He took some old film of firemen going to fires, cut it up, and pasted it back together in a different sequence. He also added some new film shot in the studio to tie each scene to the next and to make it all into a story.

Porter called this film *The Life of an American Fireman.* By moving the camera around and through a burning house

Edwin S. Porter's 1903 Western The Great Train Robbery *used every camera and editing trick known at that time. The film's chase scenes, getaways, and switching of scenes thrilled audiences.*

erected in his studio, Porter was able to show the fire fighters racing to the fire, the helpless victims about to be engulfed in flames, a fire fighter climbing a ladder, flames getting closer to the children in the house, and finally a fire fighter carrying them to safety. This was a dramatic change in movies, and people lined up to see this exciting new kind of silent motion picture.

Porter's next film, *The Great Train Robbery*, further advanced the development of motion pictures. The film ran for fourteen minutes and contained the first chase scene that movie audiences had ever watched. The chase scene was another important departure from standard moviemaking techniques. Porter not only arranged the chase in the most interesting order but he also moved the camera back and forth between scenes to show what was happening in different places at the same time. Porter showed the outlaws making their getaway from the train, for example, then cut back to the sheriff's posse mounting up for the chase. He continued to switch from scenes of the outlaws to scenes of the posse gaining on them until the audience was caught up in the action. This was thrilling new entertainment. Motion pictures were back in demand again. Porter used all of the editing and camera tricks known up to that time to make this film. It was a huge success, and Porter's style was copied everywhere.

A Nickel at a Time

The growing popularity of movies increased the need for a place to show them. It did not take long for theaters to appear. The first theater designed solely for motion pictures opened in Pittsburgh, Pennsylvania, in 1905. Called a nickelodeon because the price of admission was a nickel, it was a big step up from the variety houses where movies had been shown until then. The Pittsburgh nickelodeon had 199 seats and boasted a twenty-minute program of films. The opening night attraction was *The Great Train Robbery*, and the new theater made twenty-two dollars. Soon, it was bringing in one thousand dollars each week, a nickel at a time.

A Chaotic Industry

Nickelodeons quickly sprang up in all the major American cities. By 1907, there were three thousand, and three years later, there were more than ten thousand. In 1910 alone, more than two million people a day visited a nickelodeon. Filmmakers could not keep up with the demand for new films.

Despite the incredible success of the nickelodeons, many filmmakers still feared that motion pictures were just a fad and that the public would again tire of them. This fear, and the high demand for films, prompted some moviemakers to steal films and to copy patented movie cameras and projectors. Edison, Melies, and the Lumieres lost thousands of dollars during this time to people who stole their ideas. Angry that their ideas were being used without permission, Edison and the others decided to strike back. Edison hired a law firm to sue his competitors for using his inventions without his approval. Small and large companies alike often took matters into their own hands and hired people to raid other film company warehouses and steal back their films. The industry erupted in chaos. Employ-

A scene from D.W. Griffith's Birth of a Nation. *By 1915, when this movie was released, "two-reeler" motion pictures lasting forty minutes were standard.*

ees stole equipment and films to sell to their competitors. Movie sets were destroyed and production crews beaten up. At one point, representatives of the Lumiere company actually fled New York in a small boat and floated in the harbor until a French ocean liner picked them up.

The chaos finally came to a halt on January 1, 1909, when the major U.S. film companies formed the Motion Pictures Patents Company (MPPC). The MPPC was based in New York and was made up of the companies holding all of the patents for motion picture cameras, projectors, and film.

The Birth of Hollywood

The MPPC became the most powerful force in the motion picture industry because it could refuse to sell equipment or material to anyone. For a short time, the MPPC had exclusive control of all films. The small, independent filmmakers were being shoved out of the business by lawsuits and "enforcers" hired to make sure that equipment and film were being bought only from the MPPC. The enforcers used the same strong-arm tactics the studios had earlier used with each other. Finally, in desperation, most of the independents fled the East Coast. Several found their way to Southern California. Just outside Los Angeles, they found a perfect filming location. Within an hour's drive of the city, they had a desert, a mountain range, farm country, and a scenic ocean view. Real estate was cheap, and the sun always shined. It was also close enough to the Mexican border that they could slip across and hide from the MPPC when the need arose. These independent film producers flourished in their new location. The MPPC lost control of the industry, and in 1917 the organization was disbanded. The growing companies all relocated to the West Coast, and Hollywood was born.

As the industry grew, new names became prominent in the motion picture industry. D.W. Griffith, an actor turned producer, was one of the first to make his mark. He came to be known as the father of motion pictures. He was not afraid to try new techniques in making his movies, and he is responsible for many filmmaking innovations.

Innocence and Purity

Although movies with plots had been around for fifteen years, Griffith brought new life into motion pictures by creating a heightened sense of drama and suspense in his films. Griffith's "saved-in-the-nick-of-time" scenes became his trademark. He would cut between scenes of the hero or heroine in terrible danger and scenes of people racing to their rescue. To the audience, it seemed that the character would surely be killed before the rescuers arrived. But the rescuers always did manage to arrive just in time.

Griffith also became well known for the length of his films. Many of his movies were five times longer than most others produced at the time. *The Lonely Villa*, made in 1909, lasted nearly forty minutes and had to be shown on two separate reels. The studios laughed at him, saying the public would never sit still for a movie that long. They insisted it be released as a two-part film, but when it was shown, the audiences demanded to see the second part immediately. By the time his two-hour *Birth of a Nation* was released in 1915, "two-reelers" lasting forty minutes were the standard.

Griffith also set the tone of innocence and purity that marked the early drama and romance movies. His leading ladies included Mary Pickford, known for her "girl next door" roles; glamour-

girl Florence Lawrence; and tragic heroines Lillian and Dorothy Gish.

Like all silent film stars, Pickford, Lawrence, and the Gishes excelled at pantomime. They had to because the only words in any silent film were written on cards flashed between the scenes. Since they could not speak, the actors had to exaggerate their facial expressions and body movements. To show surprise, the actors opened their eyes wide. To show anger, they squinched their faces in a scowl. When they were sad, they did not just cry but gushed tears. Thick layers of makeup enhanced facial features so that audiences could see their expressions more clearly. Large and flamboyant body movements helped express what their characters were feeling. To show fright, the actors shrank from the camera. Villains towered over cowering victims. When bad news arrived, the actor wilted in a great show of distress. These were the quali-

Since words in the early silent films were flashed on cards between scenes, film stars like Lillian and Dorothy Gish (above) had to excel at pantomime and exaggerated facial expressions.

ties that brought great fortune to silent film stars, including Griffith's romantic leading ladies.

Search for Style

As Griffith's reputation for making films of drama and romance soared, other moviemakers searched for their own style. Mack Sennett, a director, found his place in the industry with slapstick comedy. Sennett opened his own filmmaking company, called Keystone Studios, with twenty-five hundred dollars and a dream of making comedies. Sennett's Keystone Kops, known for their zany behavior and fast-paced, pie-in-the-face antics, were an instant success.

Two of Sennett's stars were Fatty Arbuckle and Buster Keaton. Arbuckle, with his boyish face, huge waistline, and acrobatic skills, quickly became one of the country's favorite comedians. Keaton

Buster Keaton (above), seen here in Go West *(1925), was one of director Mack Sennett's most famous slapstick-comedy actors. Another one of Sennett's stars was Fatty Arbuckle (below, far right), seen here as one of the Keystone Kops, known for their wild, slapstick comedy. Keaton, too, was one of the Keystone Kops (fifth from right).*

entered the film industry in 1917 with the help of Arbuckle. Keaton was known for his portrayal of a loner caught in the madness of modern life who manages to triumph over every disaster. As popular as Arbuckle and Keaton were, they were soon outshone by Sennett's greatest contribution to the screen— Charlie Chaplin.

The Stars Are Born

Chaplin was a not-too-successful stage actor when Sennett asked him to join the Keystone Kops. After going to work for Sennett, Chaplin quickly rose to the top of the film world. Audiences adored his genius in the art of mime and his boundless imagination. But most of all,

Movie producer Carl Laemmle made actress Florence Lawrence (above) a movie star and a household name.

At this time, performers' names did not appear in any movie credits. But audiences had their favorite stars anyway and made up names for them. Mary Pickford became known as Little Mary. G.M. Anderson, famous for his good-guy cowboy roles, was called Bronco Billy after the character he played in a movie. Movie producer Carl Laemmle thought this public adoration would mean dollars in his pocket if he could advertise that his films featured the public's favorite performers. To gain public attention, Laemmle stole Florence Lawrence, Biograph Studio's main female star. Laemmle started a rumor that the "Biograph girl" had been killed in an accident, then quickly sent out a press report denying her death. Laemmle then announced that his studio had just signed the Biograph girl, Florence Lawrence. Laemmle invited the public to meet Lawrence the next day at the opening of her new picture. The public thronged to the train station to wait for her train, shouting her no longer secret name.

they loved to watch the character he called "the little tramp." The tramp wore a derby hat, baggy pants, and tight-fitting coat. He sported a toothbrush mustache and carried a bamboo cane. His shuffling walk, nervous smile, twirling cane, and formal gestures endeared him to moviegoers worldwide. Theater owners held Chaplin look-alike contests, stores sold Chaplin toys, and grown men bought Chaplin canes to twirl. All this attention boosted Chaplin's salary to levels never before experienced by a movie star. He was the first of the stars to become a millionaire, and his popularity marked another change. For the first time in film history, audiences cared more about the stars than the stories. Plot took a secondary role in what was to become the new star system.

Millionaire Stars

Other studios soon followed Laemmle's lead, releasing the names of their star performers. As the producers had feared, the most popular stars began demanding big pay raises. In the earliest days of motion pictures, all performers earned five dollars a day, no matter what role they played. Salaries had grown slightly, but not to the legendary figures that the star system made possible. Mary Pickford, swashbuckler Douglas Fairbanks, Sr., and glamourous Gloria Swanson soon joined Chaplin on the millionaire list.

Many moviegoers found the intense gaze of actor Rudolph Valentino attractive. When Valentino died suddenly in 1926, thousands of people attended his funeral.

Although the stars demanded high salaries, the studios still made money. Any film that starred one of the big-name actors was a sure money-maker because the public would flock to the movie to see its favorite star. The studios also reaped an additional benefit from the stars' popularity. Theater owners who wanted to show films featuring the stars were forced to rent a group of movies, many featuring unknown performers, from the studios. This way, studios ensured that all of the movies they produced would be shown.

Sex Appeal

Many stars became so popular that their every move was watched by the public. This started another new business—the fan magazine. Thousands of people bought these new magazines that were devoted to photographs and stories about the private lives of the stars. Movie studios produced postcards, posters, and photographs to sell to an eager public. Women all over the country copied the makeup and hairstyles of their favorite actresses.

Some of the stars attracted a huge following. Rudolph Valentino, a former gardener, rocketed to stardom with his sex appeal, his exotic tango dancing, and his smoldering stare. When Valentino died suddenly in 1926, thousands of screaming, hysterical women attended his funeral, and crowds lined up for eleven blocks to view his body.

The motion pictures had come a long way from the early "flickers" to the million-dollar spectaculars of the silent era. Many stars were burning bright, but many others were destined to dim with the coming of the "talkies."

Pictures That Talk

From the beginning, sound and pictures were meant to go together. Even with silent films, people found ingenious ways to add music and sound effects to the flickering pictures. But coordinating these various elements was difficult, and the sound and pictures rarely matched. So when inventors finally found a way to marry sound and pictures, a new era in filmmaking was born. The invention of sound technology changed the public's expectations of movies and drew people further into the world of film.

Sound Accompanies Films

The earliest sound in movies came not from inventors but from smart business-people looking for new ways to hold the interest of audiences. Theater owners played music and added sound effects as the pictures were projected.

Music was essential in setting the mood for movie audiences. Smaller movie theaters usually had a single piano, while larger ones had full orchestras performing with the film. The size of the orchestra also depended on the type of film being shown. When the silent epic *Birth of a Nation* premiered in 1915, seventy members of the Los Angeles Symphony Orchestra were hired to accompany the film. This movie rated a huge orchestra because it was the longest and most expensive movie to date.

In addition to music, many larger theaters provided special effects to enhance the film. These effects were often supplied by a drummer who used drums, blocks of wood, and whistles to provide the clatter of horse hooves, the slamming of doors, and bird whistles. Other theaters built more elaborate systems that supplied a wider range of effects. The sound of horse hooves on a paved street, for example, was produced by pounding coconut shells on marble slabs. Sandpaper rubbed on blocks simulated the sound of steam from a train, exhaust from a car, or the splash of water.

Audiences enjoyed the background music and sound effects added by theater owners. But inventors like Edison and Dickson thought they could do even better. In 1896, Edison and Dickson developed a machine that could link speech with pictures and called it a Kinetophone. The Kinetophone consisted of a Kinetoscope and a phonograph. The viewer watched moving pictures through the Kinetoscope. The Kinetoscope was attached to a phonograph. A pair of long tubes reached from the phonograph to the viewer's ears. In this way, Dickson and Edison brought sound to their motion pictures.

Talking Pictures

Kinetophones were placed in penny arcades around the country. Although they provided audiences with the world's first talking pictures, these machines failed miserably. Edison was unable to match the words spoken by the actors on the phonograph record with the movement of their lips on the screen. The effect of seeing an actor speak and then hearing the words moments later distracted and confused audiences. They disliked the Kinetophone and showed their dislike by booing the pictures and demanding their money back. This reaction forced Edison to give up the idea of making talking films.

A Breakthrough

Edison's difficulties did not deter a young American scientist named Lee De Forest. De Forest had worked for a number of years on an idea for projecting sound loudly and clearly. He knew that eventually someone would find a way to match pictures and sound. And when that happened, movie theaters would need a way of making the sound loud enough for everyone in the theater to hear. De Forest found a way to do that. He invented the vacuum tube and the loudspeaker. These devices made it possible to record and broadcast sound clearly and loudly.

De Forest sold his inventions to the Western Electric Company, whose engineers had been looking for the secret to matching pictures with sound. The company had developed a device that would do the job. Called a Vitaphone, the machine was powered by two motors. One motor moved the film through the pro-

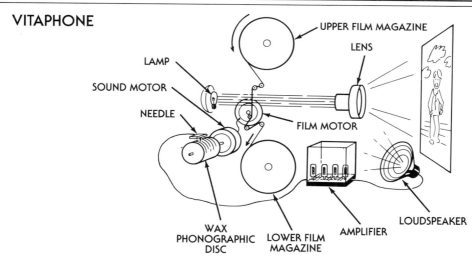

VITAPHONE

UPPER FILM MAGAZINE
LENS
LAMP
SOUND MOTOR
NEEDLE
FILM MOTOR
WAX PHONOGRAPHIC DISC
LOWER FILM MAGAZINE
AMPLIFIER
LOUDSPEAKER

The Vitaphone was the first device to synchronize sound with pictures. With the Vitaphone, the words spoken by the actors perfectly match the movement of their lips on the screen. The device is powered by two perfectly synchronized motors. One motor moves the film through the projector.

The other turns a phonographic wax disc that contains the sound of the actors' voices. The motors start and stop the film and sound at exactly the same time. The amplifier picks up the sound and sends it through a loudspeaker and into the audience.

This photograph, taken in 1925, shows an Oregon farm family listening to their "receiving set," an early name for radio.

jector, while the other turned a wax phonograph disc. The motors ensured that the sounds and pictures started and stopped at the same time. The results were perfectly matched sound and pictures. With the help of De Forest's loudspeaker to project sound, the technology was now available to produce talking motion pictures. But no studio was interested.

The motion picture industry had invested too much money in silent films to willingly switch to talking pictures. Silent films had become a $2.5-billion-a-year industry, making it one of the largest industries in the world. Production stages, studios, and theaters were designed for silent movies. In order to produce talking movies, special studios would have to be built. To show the talkies, theaters would have to be equipped with sound systems. Studios and theater owners were making huge profits from silent films and had a strong incentive to keep the movies speechless. But that did not last. The motion picture industry was able to ignore sound production for several years. But in 1920, a new invention called radio came along, killing the appeal of silent film.

Radio Kills the Silent Film

Radio was an immediate success. Statistics show how quickly people accepted the invention. By 1922, three million homes had radios. In 1924 the manufacture of radios had become a $50-million-a-year industry. In 1925, the number of homes with radios had swelled to fifty million.

By 1926, the silent movie industry was declining because of radio. People no longer had to leave their homes for entertainment, and they could enjoy music, comedy, or drama simply by turning a dial. Although movies had what radio lacked—pictures—radio offered a new novelty not found in movies—sound.

The Warner Brothers film production company was one of the first to feel the impact of radio. Warner Brothers was a small studio started in 1903 by four brothers—Harry, Albert, Sam, and Jack Warner. From the beginning, the business had struggled to overcome financial problems. As movie attendance dwindled, the young company was on the edge of bankruptcy. It needed a new gimmick to sell its films. Out of desperation, Warner Brothers became the first film studio to gamble on sound.

Warner Brothers Makes Beautiful Music

Upon hearing of Western Electric's Vitaphone device, Sam Warner traveled to New York for a demonstration. He was awed. Later he told friends, "I could not believe my own ears." Warner Brothers quickly bought the system and began producing its first sound feature, *Don Juan*. This film did not have any spoken dialogue, but it did have a musical score played on the Vitaphone. In addition, Sam Warner recorded a series of concerts performed by the New York Philharmonic Orchestra to show before the motion picture.

As production proceeded, costs soared. Warner Brothers had budgeted fifty thousand dollars for the silent version of *Don Juan*, a story about a man who seduced women. By the time pro-

duction was complete, the company had spent three million dollars to hire the orchestra, record sound, and refit one theater with the equipment necessary to project the sound. Warner Brothers was deeply in debt, and if the film failed, so would the company.

Don Juan premiered on August 6, 1926. It was an immediate success. Reviewers praised it as a "thrilling" musical program. The audience was so impressed with how the music matched the movements of the musicians that they gave the presentation a standing ovation. More important for the Warners, the film was also a financial success. The movie earned twenty-nine thousand dollars in its first week, more than had ever been earned by a single theater in history. The show ran for eight months at the theater, and 500,000 people went to see it.

Despite the film's success, almost no one thought that sound pictures would actually lead to talking pictures. Most people assumed the Vitaphone would be used to add musical scores to films. The *New York Times* praised the Vitaphone as a way to bring opera to small and remote cities. Even the Warner brothers argued about adding speech to films. Sam Warner thought the new system could be used to film and screen Broadway plays. His brother Harry responded, "Who the hell wants to hear actors talk?"

Even though they were unsure of talking movies, the Warner brothers knew the public wanted sound films. In May 1927, the company announced plans to produce a full-length sound picture called *The Jazz Singer*. The studio chose the popular singer and stage actor Al Jolson to play the role of a young singer who leaves his family to sing on

Broadway. The Warners thought audiences would flock to theaters to hear Jolson sing in the movie.

The film included six songs by Jolson and two short dialogues that had been recorded by accident. Warner Brothers had not intended to include any speaking parts in the film. But twice during filming, Jolson made comments before beginning his songs. The microphone, turned on to record his singing, caught the brief snatches of conversation. Sam Warner liked the dialogue enough to keep it in the film.

The film premiered to a packed house on October 6, 1927. As Warner Brothers had anticipated, most people had come to hear Jolson sing. But it was not his singing that truly thrilled his fans—it was his talking. The audience was mesmerized when Jolson looked down at them from the movie screen and said, "Wait a minute, you ain't heard nothin' yet!" With this one short line, the era of talking films was born.

The End of an Era

After seeing and hearing *The Jazz Singer,* the public demanded sound. Even though early talking pictures were plagued with technical problems, audiences loved them. In early films the wax phonograph records used for sound tracks often produced a background hiss loud enough to drown out the dialogue. But even when audiences could not understand the words, they still loved the novelty of talking pictures.

The era of talking films was born with The Jazz Singer, *starring Al Jolson. After this, sound movies rapidly replaced the silent films.*

Edison's experiments in sound allowed later improvements.

Fan mail filled with praises for the talking actors poured into the studios. During the first years of sound films, the studios received thirty-two million fan letters per week.

Unlike the general public, most newspaper movie reviewers hated the early talking pictures. These critics complained about the lack of action and artistry in the talkies. One critic described the talking movie as "merely a novelty to be used sparingly" and predicted that talkies were "doomed to failure." But filmmakers were convinced that the novelty of talking pictures was all that was needed to bring audiences back to the theaters, and they were right. During the early days, patrons flocked to theaters no matter how bad the movie.

Sound saved the movie industry, which continued to thrive even through the depression years. During the depression, when thousands of people were out of work and few could afford any type of luxury, the number of moviego-

ers jumped from fifty-seven million a week to ninety-seven million. In just two years, the public's demand for talkies forced studios to create sound pictures and install sound equipment in theaters across the nation. By 1929, the major studios had spent thirty-seven million dollars wiring their theaters for sound.

Death of the Silent Film Star

As studio executives focused their attention on producing sound movies, terror swept through the world of the silent film stars. Suddenly, stars who were used to demanding huge salaries had to prove their worth all over again. Many never made the transition. For them, the advent of sound was the death of their careers. Those who wanted to keep their jobs had to prove they could do something that most people did every day—talk.

Silent-film star Gloria Swanson had to adapt to "the talkies."

The changes sweeping Hollywood were evident on March 29, 1928, when the United Artists film studio sponsored a radio broadcast to prove that its best-known actors could talk. These actors included Mary Pickford, Gloria Swanson, Douglas Fairbanks, Sr., John Barrymore, and Charlie Chaplin. These were the legends of the era, but they all were as nervous as unknown actors as they waited for their chance to prove they had a voice. People across the country listened to the radio program to hear their favorite stars. Films were even stopped in movie theaters so that audiences could also hear the radio broadcast.

Stop the Broadcast

The show was a disaster. The speeches were long and boring, and audiences soon became restless. In some theaters, patrons yelled catcalls at the radio. Newspaper articles said much of the show was greeted with "moans and boos." Some theater owners had to shut down for the night and refund ticket money. Others simply stopped the broadcast and returned to their normal movie program. In the weeks following the broadcast, rumors circulated that the stars had used other actors to do their talking for them. The rumors later proved to be false. But the atmosphere of dread continued to spread through the acting community as stars waited to see if they had the right voice for talking pictures.

Desperation took hold, even among lesser-known actors. One young starlet named Peg Entwhistle, fearing she would be unable to make the transition to talking movies, jumped to her death from the famous Hollywood sign.

John Barrymore, seen here portraying a swashbuckling pirate, was one of several well-known actors who made the conversion from silent to talking films.

Accents Unpopular

Other careers were ended less dramatically but just as swiftly by the talkies. One of the most famous victims of sound was John Gilbert. Gilbert, known as the Great Lover, was a leading heartthrob during the silent era. At the peak of his career, he earned $250,000 a film. But when sound came to movies, Gilbert's career was over. Audiences laughed at his squeaky, weak voice.

Stars with accents were also unpopular. Norma Talmadge, who played glamour-girl roles in silent films, saw her career come to an end in 1930 when she was only thirty-five years old. Audiences laughed at her strong Brooklyn accent when she played an eighteenth-century French aristocrat in *Du Barry, Woman of Passion*. Her sister Constance, also a silent film star, advised her to "leave them while you're looking good." Both Talmadge sisters retired from the screen soon after.

The Perfect Way

Foreign-born star Pola Negri, who had built her reputation on her exotic looks, earned six thousand dollars a week playing silent film roles as a sultry seductress. But as the popularity of talkies grew, Negri was unable to find work. Although her dark hair and dark eyes had attracted a loyal following, her heavy German accent made her voice unintelligible to audiences. As with most other actors who had strong accents, the talkies ended Negri's career.

An exception to this trend was Greta Garbo, one of the biggest stars of the silent screen. Garbo, who was born in Sweden, was famous for her roles as a fragile, romantic heroine in silent films. She also feared that her fans would desert her when they heard her accent for the first time. For this reason, Garbo was one of the last silent stars to make a talking movie. In 1930, she starred in

Movies heavily influenced the way people lived. When Clark Gable wore no undershirt in It Happened One Night *(1934), undershirt sales dropped 40 percent.*

Greta Garbo feared her fans would desert her when they heard her Swedish accent. But the success of Anna Christie *(1930) proved Garbo would remain a star.*

Anna Christie, a film about a Swedish immigrant. In this film, Garbo found the perfect way to introduce her Swedish accent, and her fans loved it. *Anna Christie* was advertised simply with the slogan "Garbo Talks!" The public was as taken with her voice as they had been with her silent performances. One reviewer described her voice as "rich, full . . . [and] smoky." Garbo made the transition smoothly to sound and continued to be one of the leading ladies of the sound era.

Another star who successfully made the transition was Ronald Coleman. Like John Gilbert, Coleman had been a silent screen leading man. But unlike Gilbert, Coleman's debut in talkies showed that he had the right voice. Coleman had a deep voice that suited his roles, and his fans loved to hear him talk. Crowds besieged Coleman after the May 1929 premiere of his first talking film, an action-adventure film called *Bulldog Drummond.*

New Fads

The public was quick to forget its silent film idols and embrace the new talking stars. During the silent days, fans had worshiped their movie idols from afar.

The silent stars were considered remote, untouchable, and far removed from daily life. But sound films changed everything. Talking movies were more realistic than silents, which depended on elaborate pantomimes. Sound movies, on the other hand, featured performers who walked, talked, and acted like real people. Audiences saw these stars as both role models and idols, and fans began to imitate their favorite stars.

Fashion Trends

The new film stars influenced the way Americans dressed, talked, and decorated their homes. When women smoked on-screen, the idea of women smoking in public became acceptable and even glamourous. When suave leading man Clark Gable took off his shirt and revealed he did not wear an undershirt in his film *It Happened One Night,* the sale of undershirts dropped 40 percent. When a film star adopted a new dress style, that style could be seen on the streets in a few weeks.

Garbo especially influenced fashion trends. She often wore hats in her roles, and American women avidly copied every hat style she wore. Garbo's movies popularized the pillbox hat, the turban, and the beret. When a fan magazine announced she wore trench coats in public, trench coats became a craze.

Movie-inspired fads reached a new height in 1940 with a Brazilian actress named Carmen Miranda. She dressed spectacularly, even for Hollywood. In all of her performances, she wore enormous bunches of fruit on her head, shoulders, and wrists. Her fans soon donned artificial fruit to look like their

The Carmen Miranda fad of the 1940s motivated fans to decorate their homes—and bodies—with artificial fruit.

idol. In addition, children played with Carmen Miranda dolls, while their parents decorated the house with artificial fruit. Banana cooky jars, banana earrings, fruit bracelets, and cherry necklaces swept the nation from 1940 to 1945 when Miranda starred in movies such as *That Night in Rio* and *Down Argentine Way,* in which she played a lighthearted singer and dancer.

The various fads that swept the nation show the tremendous interest the American public had in motion pictures. People idolized the stars, and theaters were filled every week with fans anxious to see every movie released by their favorite actors. During the 1930s and 1940s, the average person went to the theater at least twice a week, and the number of theaters was growing rapidly to meet the public's demand. The motion picture industry was entering its heyday.

The Golden Age to the Television Age

Once motion pictures found their voice, the industry entered a golden age. The public was hungry for new movies, and Hollywood provided audiences with an abundance of star-filled films. This was the era of extravagant, costly films. Movie screens were filled with spectacular musicals featuring hundreds of dancers and elaborate dramatic productions. During this time, the studios also gained tremendous power. Eventually, the studios controlled every aspect of the motion picture industry from the admission price of theater tickets to the lives of screen stars. For twenty years, the movie studios were virtual dictators.

Power of the Studios

Under the emerging studio system, the film industry was able to mass-produce films. The system was introduced by a businessman named Thomas Ince. Ince developed the studio system at his film production company in Culver City, California. He ran the studio, called Inceville, like a manufacturing business. He organized teams of creative and administrative personnel who worked together to produce movies.

Ince's idea soon caught on with all of the studio executives. They found this system allowed them to produce films more quickly. In the early years of motion pictures, studio executives kept tight control over all of the movies made at their film companies. But, like Ince, they soon found they were making so many productions that they could not handle all of the details alone. So, instead of personally directing each movie, the companies established a separate production unit for every film. Each unit was headed by a manager, known as the producer, who was responsible for making the film to the company's specifications.

In addition, the companies made sure they owned all of the raw material necessary to produce a film. Each studio kept a crew of directors, actors, technicians, and costume designers under contract. These people were allowed to work for only one studio, and they were to be available whenever needed. When the studio was ready to begin work on a new film, the producer simply had to look through the company's personnel list and choose who he or she wanted. Sets and costumes were provided by woodworking and costume shops located on the studio's lot.

Each studio also had a series of permanent sets on its grounds. Typical sets included a Japanese village, an Irish settlement town, Swiss chalets, and log cabins. With these sets, a director could film in a variety of exotic locations just by moving the camera a few feet.

These innovations enabled studios to produce a large number of movies very rapidly. The studio system seemed to be ideal for production companies

Thomas Ince ran his studio like a manufacturing company.

trying to meet the growing demand for motion pictures. And the system paid off. Studio executives quickly became rich by following Ince's lead. By 1937, Louis B. Mayer, head of Metro-Goldwyn-Mayer (MGM), was making more money than anyone else in the United States. His salary of $1.29 million that year was ten times greater than that of the president of the United States.

Lives Under Contract

As the power of the studios increased, so did their hold on the movie stars. The stars were the products that the studios sold. Each studio maintained an array of celebrities and virtually controlled their lives. Every star in Hollywood was under contract with a studio. It was not long before each studio became known for its set of performers and the types of films it made. MGM, for example, produced spectacular

movies filled with casts of hundreds. Its stars included leading man Clark Gable; Judy Garland, often cast as the "girl next door"; Mickey Rooney, who often portrayed bright and eager college students; and James Stewart, who played good-guy heroes.

In contrast, Warner Brothers specialized in tough, realistic dramas. Its actors were rugged men and women who could survive any hardship. These included streetwise Lauren Bacall, loner Humphrey Bogart, tough-guy gangster James Cagney, and swashbuckling Errol Flynn.

Most contracts tied the actors to a studio for at least seven years, and during that period the studios owned them. The contracts controlled all aspects of their lives. Sultry leading lady Joan Crawford, for example, had a contract specifying the time she had to go to bed each night. Walter Pidgeon, who started

Like other actresses of her day, Joan Crawford was owned by the studio. Her contract even specified the time she had to go to bed at night.

Lauren Bacall (right) was one of the Warner Brothers stars who acted in tough, realistic dramas. Others included Humphrey Bogart, James Cagney, and Errol Flynn.

his movie career as a singer, agreed to a clause that forbade him to sing tenor because he might strain his baritone voice. One starlet who liked boxing was forbidden to yell during boxing matches because it might damage her voice.

Harsh Conditions

Contracts also specified the number of movies an actor had to make each year. But working conditions were usually not outlined in the agreement. Studios interested in making as many films as possible made the performers work long hours under harsh conditions.

An actor's day usually started at 6 A.M. and lasted late into the night. Often, the grueling schedules would continue for months at a time as performers went from film to film. Sometimes, shooting on one picture would end the day before work began on a new project. While working for Warner Brothers, for example, James Cagney acted in twenty films in a two-year period. Other actors kept equally hectic schedules. In 1930, Clark Gable appeared in fourteen movies for MGM.

If a performer refused to make a movie, or complained about working conditions, he or she was suspended without pay. And the suspension time was added on to the length of the star's contract. While suspended, performers were legally barred from working for other studios. Studios used suspensions to maintain control of the performers. In this way, the studios could keep actors under contract for much longer than seven years.

From Moviemaking to Ticket Taking

In addition to owning the production companies and the stars, most studios owned theater chains. This guaranteed that each studio had a ready market for its films. For example, theaters owned by MGM played only MGM movies. Because they were controlled by the stu-

Clark Gable was one of many actors in the 1920s and 1930s who kept a hectic schedule. In 1930, he appeared in fourteen movies for MGM.

dios, theaters were forced to show all of the movies produced by its owner, regardless of quality.

Studios also enforced the practice of block booking—renting films as a package rather than individually—which was started during the silent era. If the theaters wanted one film with a major star, they were forced to rent five or ten other films with lesser-known actors.

By 1946, the studios controlled the entire motion picture industry. Because they regulated everything down to the minimum admission price of theater tickets, the production companies were making incredible profits. In 1946, the total industry made nearly two billion dollars. This was the industry's best year, but the end of the era was near. Within four years, the studios' hold on the film business would be over.

Death of the Studios

The first blow to the reign of the studios came in 1948 when the United States Supreme Court ruled that studios could not own theaters. The court decided that the practice of owning both the production and distribution units was illegal because it gave the studios a monopoly, or exclusive control, over the making and selling of movies.

Because of the ruling, the studios had to sell their theater chains. The production companies soon found, to their dismay, that there was more money in exhibiting films than in producing them. The loss of the theaters cost the studios millions of dollars in profit. The change also meant that production companies had to think more about the quality of their films. Once theater owners were free of studio control, they began to select the movies they believed would sell best. This meant that not every film produced would be sold.

A New Threat

At the same time the studios were reeling from the court decision, a new threat appeared. This one—the invention of television—abruptly ended the movie industry's golden age. As in the past, the industry found itself struggling to win back its audience. But television was a formidable enemy.

Television was an instant success. By 1950, twenty-five million families had television sets in their homes. Television offered viewers the enjoyment of films with the added advantage of not having to leave the house. Television's impact on films was swift. Motion picture ticket sales fell as Americans chose to tune in to shows on their televisions. By 1952, the number of people who attended cinemas had dropped from ninety million a week to fifty million. As audiences shrank, theaters began to close. Between 1948 and 1956, the number of U.S. theaters fell from twenty thousand to ten thousand. Even the world's most famous movie palace, the Roxy Theater in New York City, fell victim to the trend. Its chandeliers, organ, curtains, carpets, and air conditioning equipment were offered free to anyone who would cart them away.

In an effort to reduce cost, the studios began making drastic changes. The Hollywood companies, which had survived the depression without reducing their work force, laid off twelve thousand people. Next, the studios cut back on production. By 1960, the number of films produced by major studios per year had fallen from three hundred to only seventy.

Finally, the studios were forced to release stars from contracts. Instead of owning the performers, studios began to hire them on a movie-by-movie basis. The end of the old system seemed near when MGM was forced to release its most popular star, Clark Gable, in 1954 because it could no longer afford to pay his salary of $520,000 a year. By 1955, no star was under a studio contract.

As audiences continued to dwindle, filmmakers became more innovative. Remembering how sound had saved movies from the threat of radio, the industry began looking for a new gimmick to save itself from television.

Pictures with Depth

One of the first innovations tried was three-dimensional, or 3-D, movies. These movies promised audiences experiences that television could not match. Posters for the first 3-D movie, *Bwana Devil,* vowed the movie would "put a lion in your lap." The 3-D process is based on the fact that when viewing an object, each eye sees a slightly different picture. The left eye sees a little more around the left side of an object, and the right eye sees more to the right. To record these two different views and produce a 3-D movie, two shots of each scene are taken with two different cameras. One camera photographs what the right eye would see, and the other is placed about two inches to the left to photograph what the left eye would see. The two images are projected on top of each other on the movie screen.

In order to make the three-dimensional film come to life, spectators must wear special glasses that unscramble the double image. The glasses enable a viewer's right eye to see one shot and the left eye the other. The brain fuses the two images into a single picture that appears to have depth. This is what gives viewers the impression that actors literally walk off the screen.

When *Bwana Devil* premiered in December 1952, few major studios took 3-D films seriously. But when the low-budget movie earned fifteen million dollars, 3-D films seemed to be the way to beat television. Audiences and movie reviewers were enthusiastic about the new movies. The industry magazine *Film*

Daily called *Bwana Devil* "the most . . . outstanding movie of the moment." One reviewer predicted that in the future, audiences would demand all movies be made in 3-D.

To Save the Movies

People loved the novelty of the new technology, and it quickly became a fad. Three-dimensional comic books were published, and fan magazines began printing 3-D pictures of the stars. During 1953 alone, 100 million people attended 3-D movies. Every theater showing the new movies reported long wait-

---

3-D MOVIES

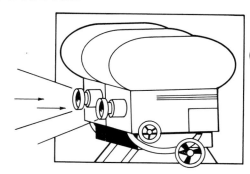

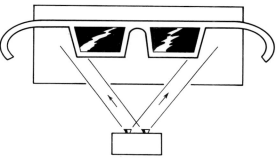

In three-dimensional movies, actors seem to literally leap off the movie screen and into the theater. To create this effect, moviemakers mimic real-life vision, in which each eye sees a slightly different image. Based on this principle, moviemakers use two motion picture cameras to shoot the movie. The distance between the two camera lenses is about the same as the distance between a person's eyes. This makes it possible for the cameras to photograph an object the way each human eye would see it.

When a 3-D movie is shown in the theater, the two images are projected on top of one another. The movie appears blurry and unfocused, as though each figure has a double shadow. To make the film come to life, viewers must wear special glasses. These glasses, through special filters, help the viewer's eyes separate the double images so that each eye sees a different image. The brain fuses the two images into one complete, three-dimensional picture that appears to jump off the screen.

ing lines. One theater owner called 3-D the "most fabulous thing we've ever seen."

For one year, 3-D seemed to save the movies. But then the novelty of three-dimensional films died. Audiences who loved the 3-D effect hated the special glasses they had to wear. Many people complained of headaches and dizziness from wearing the special glasses. By 1954, 3-D movies had lost their audience.

Color and the Big Screen

As three-dimensional productions lost their appeal, studios turned to another idea—color—in hopes of saving the industry. Color films had been possible since the invention of motion pictures. But color photography was an expensive process. As long as black-and-white films made huge profits, studios were not interested in producing the more expensive color films. The threat of television in the 1950s rekindled interest in color, however. Since all television programs were black-and-white, studios thought that by offering color, they might lure viewers away from their television sets.

The basic principles of color photography—which also formed the basis for color motion pictures—were discovered by Isaac Newton more than three hundred years ago. Newton discovered that light is made up of a range of colors. In addition, he found that three of the colors of light—red, green, and blue—could be combined in different amounts to produce almost every visible color. For example, blue light and red light combined in equal amounts produce magenta. This phenomenon was then applied to film production. Color film is coated with layers of filtering material that absorb and combine red, blue, and green light to produce color pictures. This type of film is used in both still photography and in motion pictures.

One of the earliest processes for producing color motion pictures, named Technicolor, was invented in 1917. Some filmmakers experimented with the new color film, but Technicolor had too many problems to be popular. One of its major drawbacks was the poor quality of the pictures. Film reviewers called the early movies "tiresome and grainy." Because the Technicolor system used only two colors, red and green, the colors on the film were often not realistic. In these early films, the sea and sky would both appear green.

Audiences also disliked the early color, and some people complained that the bright hues caused eyestrain. If it had not been for the development of a three-color system, color films may have disappeared entirely. By 1930, Technicolor had switched to the new three-color system that used red, blue, and green filters to produce more natural colors. While the new films were superior to early color films, reaction to them was mixed.

The *New York Times* wrote that "there are some exquisite sequences of color photography, in which one enjoys the sight of the varied hues and tints." Another reviewer, after seeing *Becky Sharp*, the 1935 movie based on the novel *Vanity Fair*, was not so enthusiastic. He wrote that actors in the film were the color of "boiled salmon dipped in mayonnaise."

Even though the use of color was becoming more accepted in the late

The advent of television posed a serious threat to the motion picture industry.

1930s, it was used sparingly. Color film was still much more expensive than black-and-white, and shooting a movie in color cost 50 percent more.

Trying to Win Back the Viewers

As television's popularity grew, however, studios began producing more color films. By 1955, half of all films were in color. Audiences were interested in the color movies, but color failed to save the industry as sound had once done. People did not flock to the theaters as they had when sound was added to films. The introduction of color started no fads as the three-dimensional movies had. Most Americans still preferred to stay home and watch black-and-white shows on television. Film audiences continued to dwindle. By 1960, the number of people who attended the theaters each week fell to twenty million.

Although color did not save the in-

dustry, Hollywood continued to experiment with it, and studios produced a mixture of black-and-white and color movies throughout the 1950s. The film industry finally switched completely to color production when it had no other choice. In 1954, television stations began broadcasting a few programs in color, and by 1965, all three major television networks were broadcasting only in color. Instead of being a novelty, color production became the norm. Filmmakers had to switch to color because audiences expected it.

Even though the movies lost some of their audiences during these years, motion pictures did not lose any of their power. By the time of the golden age, producers and politicians had discovered the incredible power of movies to sway public opinion. This power was enlisted to promote a number of political and social causes, especially support of the U.S. war effort. Whenever the country went to war, the movies joined ranks to help support the cause.

Movies and War

The power and potential of movies was underestimated during the industry's infancy. But the unusual power movies possessed—to stir emotions, sway public opinion, and influence the way we live —became evident as the popularity of movies soared. The world's political leaders, for example, found motion pictures an especially valuable tool of persuasion in times of war. In the movies, complex issues were often simplified for the sake of the plot. Many political leaders who felt that the complex issues of war were too difficult for the general public to understand relied on movies to get their points across.

Support Revolution?

Few understood this tactic better in the early 1900s than Mexican general Pancho Villa. During his campaign to win control of Mexico from its ruler, Villa used films to gain American support for his cause. Villa thought that if the

Movies helped Mexican general Pancho Villa convey his revolutionary needs to the American public. Villa hoped these movies would lead to support from the U.S. government.

American public came to understand the causes he was fighting for, then the United States might support his army. He turned to motion pictures to convey his message.

Villa's Battles

On January 3, 1914, Villa signed a contract with the Mutual Film Corporation for the rights to film all of his battles. The contract stated that whenever possible, battles would be fought in daylight and at times that were convenient for the company. Villa even postponed his 1914 attack on the Mexican city of Ojinaga until a camera crew arrived.

Villa was one of the first political leaders to use movies for propaganda purposes. Propaganda is the use of information and ideas to influence opinion or support a cause. Other political leaders also developed a keen appreciation for the power of propaganda films. Among those who found them useful was the twenty-sixth U.S. president, Theodore Roosevelt. Before serving as president, Roosevelt commanded the Rough Riders, a military unit that won acclaim in the Spanish-American War. During that war, Roosevelt saw how films could stimulate public opinion. A ninety-second silent film called *Tearing Down the Spanish Flag* convinced Roosevelt of the power movies possessed. The movie showed little more than an American crowd destroying a Spanish flag. But the film drew huge crowds, stirred American patriotism and support for the war, and even incited some to reenact the destruction of the Spanish flag.

Having witnessed the power of motion pictures once, Roosevelt did not have to be persuaded that movies could again be useful in rallying support for war. Although he had stepped down from the presidency in 1909, Roosevelt remained active in efforts to bring the United States into World War I. Many Americans at the time objected to the nation's involvement in a foreign war, so the former president turned to motion pictures for help.

Roosevelt persuaded J. Stuart Blackton, director of *Tearing Down the Spanish Flag,* to produce another movie. This one was to persuade Americans to join the French and British in their war against Germany. Blackton immediately went to work on the new movie, and in 1915 he released *The Battle Cry of Peace.* The movie depicted German planes dropping bombs on New York City and German soldiers marching through the streets of Washington, D.C. The film implied that the only way the United States could have peace was by joining World War I. People who opposed American involvement in the war protested against the movie, but it was a box office success.

Supporting the War Effort

Although *Battle Cry* did not actually convince the nation to join the war, it did prompt a series of pro-war movies. One of the most popular was *The Little American,* made in 1917. The movie showed America's sweetheart, Mary Pickford, being abused and almost killed by German soldiers. Seeing their favorite star being so mistreated helped inflame public opinion. Advertising posters for the movie included a picture of the American flag, an eagle, and a gun. Emblazoned across the top of the poster was the message "For Flag and Country

Enlist Now." This movie and others like it did help convince the public to accept and even support U.S. involvement in the war.

Boosting Support

At the same time American filmmakers were trying to boost public support for the war, a group of Germans decided to make a film that would send a different message to the American public. They hired American filmmaker Robert Goldstein to produce *The Spirit of '76*, a movie that depicted Americans and Germans fighting against the British during the American Revolution. This actually never occurred, but the Germans hoped the film would persuade Americans to see the Germans as their allies and the British as their real enemy.

The movie failed, both at the box office and in its mission to weaken public support for the war. It became clear that even movies had their limits when it came to influencing public opinion. This failure apparently escaped the attention of federal authorities, who worried about the film's effect on viewers. Goldstein was arrested and convicted of producing a film hostile to the interests of the United States. The filmmaker was sentenced to ten years in prison.

Once the United States entered the war, the government was quick to enlist motion pictures in the war effort. Within a week of declaring war on Germany, the United States formed the Committee on Public Information (CPI), which was headed by journalist George Creel.

Creel saw the CPI as "a plain publicity proposition, a vast enterprise in salesmanship." His job was to make Americans war-conscious. Creel used films, posters, pamphlets, and movie stars to convince the American public of the need for making sacrifices for the war effort. The CPI opened local branches in every state. The committee also hired seventy-five thousand people to speak in movie theaters across the United States before every film. The speakers rallied public support and encouraged people to buy war bonds and conserve food and supplies.

The nation soon became swept up in Creel's campaign. Slogans started by the committee like the famous cry "Beat back the Hun!" soon became household phrases. Creel hired stars like Douglas Fairbanks, Sr., known for his adventurous hero roles, to sell bonds, and the public bought more than even Creel had hoped. The government raised twenty-three billion dollars through the sale of bonds during this time when the population had an average total annual income of only seventy billion dollars.

The CPI was active until the end of World War I. But Congress saw no reason to support a propaganda agency in peacetime. By 1919, Congress had cut funding and eliminated the CPI.

A New War

After World War I, interest in war movies waned. The world was weary of battle, and audiences wanted happier themes. Moviemakers went back to making movies designed to entertain. Musicals and westerns became popular. But in 1930, trouble began brewing in Europe again. At first, the film industry paid no attention to the growing unrest. While newspapers discussed the Spanish Civil War, the Japanese invasion of China, and Hitler's annexation of Czechoslovakia, Hollywood ignored the headlines.

Motion picture executives avoided these topics because they feared censorship, which was a growing threat. Some Americans wanted censorship that would eliminate sex and violence in films, while others were speaking out against racism and stereotypes in movies. A number of people, including many politicians, also feared the motion picture industry's power to sway public opinion in favor of war. The memories of World War I were still fresh in the minds of many people who did not want to become involved in another war. And they did not want motion pic-

tures pushing public opinion in that direction. All of this combined to create a climate of fear in the movie industry. Movie executives worried that they would be attacked for trying to stir up war. This, they thought, would give the government an excuse to begin censoring films. So most filmmakers avoided controversial subjects, including the war.

A Vocal Minority

Some producers and directors refused to be silent, however. Warner Brothers' *Confessions of a Nazi Spy*, made in 1939, marked the end of this silence. The film was based on the real-life trial of German spies operating in the United

Confessions of a Nazi Spy (1939) commented on war. Warner Brothers made the movie to avenge the murder of one of its Jewish employees.

States. These spies, according to the film, were trying to gain support for the Nazis in the United States. At one point in the film, one character turned to the camera to tell the audience it must be prepared to defend itself.

Warner Brothers made the movie in retaliation for the murder of one of its employees. In 1936, the company's German representative, Joe Kaufman, was kicked to death in a Berlin alley by a group of Nazis because he was Jewish. This murder convinced the studio it was time for the film industry to act.

The movie was a box office hit, and it stirred strong reactions. An American pro-Nazi group called the Bund sued Warner Brothers for five million dollars, claiming the film damaged the group's reputation. The film's star, Edward G. Robinson, received death threats. Nothing came of them. Overseas, where the Nazi party was more powerful, the film had deadly effects. Theater owners in Poland were hanged in their cinemas for showing the picture.

Following the Leader

Other studios soon followed Warner Brothers' lead and began producing movies supporting the war. *A Yank in the R.A.F.* (Royal Air Force), made in 1941, showed Americans going to Europe to help Great Britain win the war. The film turned out to be Twentieth Century Fox's most successful movie of the year. Audiences also responded to *I Wanted Wings*, made in 1941. Young men who watched the daring air battles staged in the movie eagerly joined the U.S. Army Air Corps.

The tone and message of these movies, their popularity, and the growing public support for U.S. intervention

When the Japanese bombed Pearl Harbor, the U.S. government relied upon the film industry to rally Americans to fight. The industry made hundreds of movies that supported the war effort.

in the war alarmed Americans who opposed this involvement. A group led by aviator Charles Lindbergh complained to Congress that the film industry was guilty of warmongering, or trying to cause a war.

Congress began investigating these accusations in September 1941. But the issue was never resolved. When Japan attacked Pearl Harbor on December 7, 1941, the congressional investigating committee adjourned without a decision.

Movies Go to War

The bombing of Pearl Harbor pushed the United States into World War II. At that point, the government again enlisted the help of the motion picture industry to rally public support. Within two weeks, the government had formed the War Activities Committee, whose purpose was to channel government suggestions for films to the movie studios. The committee proposed films that fell into five broad categories. Movies were to explain the issues of the war, describe the enemy, glorify the Allies, encourage Americans to keep up production of war supplies, and boost morale.

The industry responded by making hundreds of films supporting the war effort. Among these films was *Mrs. Miniver*, a 1942 tribute to British civilians caught in the war. The movie was a big hit in the United States and helped marshal support for the British war effort. After seeing the hardships British citizens were enduring because of the war, Americans were more willing to endure food shortages at home.

It did not take long for govern-

The brave roles that British actress Greer Garson played, such as Mrs. Miniver *(1942), symbolized British determination during World War II.*

ments to realize that not only the movie plots but also the stars themselves possessed the power of influence. British-born film star Greer Garson, for example, volunteered to return to Great Britain from Hollywood to entertain troops, but British authorities refused her offer. In her films, Garson often played roles of brave British women surviving the horrors of war. These roles became a symbol of British determination, and British authorities felt she could help the war effort more by continuing to make such films in Hollywood. Other film stars were put to work raising money for the war effort. Dorothy Lamour, known for her sexy comedies, sold $300 million worth of war bonds during World War II.

The influence of some actors was

When British prime minister Winston Churchill learned actor Laurence Olivier was filming Henry V *(1944), Churchill asked Olivier to emphasize some of Prince Hal's speeches to his troops. Churchill thought the speeches would rally British troops fighting the Axis powers during World War II.*

taken so seriously that occasionally they were asked to make changes in the characters they portrayed. One story goes that Prime Minister Winston Churchill heard that famed British actor Laurence Olivier planned to make a film version of William Shakespeare's *Henry V*. Olivier was to play the role of Prince Hal, a man who leads his weary British troops to victory against overwhelming forces. Although gallant and victorious, the character is often filled with doubt and despair over the rightness of his actions. Churchill worried about how this film and Olivier's portrayal of the character would affect his nation at a time when public morale was already very low. So Churchill, according to the story, asked Olivier to cut some of the play's most despairing moments and play up the prince's great

rallying speeches to his troops. Churchill felt this would help boost his nation's flagging morale. Olivier apparently agreed to Churchill's request. The movie was released in 1944 without the play's darkest moments.

A Realistic Picture

In an attempt to present a realistic picture of war without damaging public sentiment for the war effort, British filmmakers also developed a special kind of film referred to as a semidocumentary. These semidocumentaries were fictional stories based on real events. Often, these movies included footage of actual war scenes. Great Britain was the only country that routinely used film of real war scenes in its movies. The British flocked to theaters to see these films. One of the most popular was *In Which We Serve,* made in 1942. This film told the story of the sinking of the British ship HMS *Kelly* off the coast of Crete. Movies like this showed the harsh conditions and tragedies of the war but also depicted the importance of unity and sacrifice.

German Films Go to War

The Americans and British were not alone in their discovery of the power of films. Germany's Nazi party had been using movies since 1919 to stir public support for its efforts. German films between World War I and World War II were designed to build a strong feeling of German unity in a nation that had been devastated by its loss in World War I. During this time, Germany experienced a harsh financial depression. Many people were out of work, and prices soared. Nazi films blamed these problems on the foreign countries that had defeated Germany in the First World War. The German public, looking for someone to blame, was willing to believe the messages in the Nazi films.

As the Nazi party took control of the country, the film industry was given the responsibility of reinforcing the party's beliefs. Nazi leader Adolf Hitler believed repetition was the key to controlling the people he governed and that films could be used to accomplish this task. He wrote, "The intelligence of the masses is small. Their forgetfulness is great. They must be told the same thing thousands of times." Hitler, like

Adolf Hitler believed films were an excellent way to spread his propaganda. The Nazi party had used films since 1919 to stir public support for its causes. War films with a message became the German film industry's primary product.

other leaders during World War I and II, found films to be an excellent way to spread his messages.

The Glory of Dying

The 1933 film *Morgenrot* (Dawn) tells the story of German submarine sailors being killed in war. The film stressed the glory of dying in the service of Germany. The movie caused a furor in Great Britain's Parliament, which wanted to officially protest the film's portrayal of the British. Relations with Germany were already strained, so British officials decided against an official protest.

By 1938, the Nazi government totally controlled the German film industry, and war films with a message became the industry's chief product. One of the important films that year was Karl Ritter's *Pour le Merite,* which encouraged

contempt for democratic ideals. In it, a Nazi screams: "I hate this democracy, I hate all democracies like the plague." Other films, such as *Kopf Hoch, Johannes* (Chin Up, Johannes) were made to inspire allegiance to Nazi ideals. This movie, made in 1941, tells the story of a young man sent to a Nazi-supervised boarding school. While in school, he learns the joys of conforming to Nazi ideals. Other films, including *Jungens* (Guys), sent the message that denouncing family and friends was good for the state.

Looking Back

The power of motion pictures to influence people is used most often during wartime to stir the public to action. But in the aftermath of war, some filmmakers use movies to reflect on the issues of war. Often, these movies examine the

One of the world's first films to depict the horrors of war was All Quiet on the Western Front *(1930).*

The Deer Hunter *(1978) tells the story of a Vietnam war veteran who returns home after the fighting.*

reasons for involvement in a war, the horrors of fighting, and the long-term effects of a war on both soldiers and civilians. Whether intended or not, these films often fall into a group known as antiwar films.

One of the first antiwar films was *All Quiet on the Western Front*, released in 1930 and perhaps the most famous film in this category. Based on a German World War I novel written by journalist Erich Maria Remarque, the movie explores the author's experiences during the war. The book and film reveal the terror soldiers experience during trench warfare and the horror of week-long artillery bombardments and machine-gun assaults. The movie presented the idea that wars were often bloodbaths, with so many killed that winning did not always seem worth the price.

The Horrors of War

This was one of the first movies to take a realistic look at the horrors rather than the glories of war. It was perhaps surprising, then, that the movie was both a financial and artistic success. It also led

to worldwide debate on the necessity of war. Despite this movie's success, anti-war films were not made as often as

Coming Home *(1978) depicts the life of a Vietnam veteran whose war injuries left him paralyzed below the waist.*

other war films. In the United States, for example, antiwar films did not really become popular until after the Vietnam conflict. This war, in which thousands died, split American public opinion as no other war had before. The debate over U.S. actions in Vietnam continued long after the last American troops left that country in 1975. By 1978, several films began examining specific issues of the Vietnam fighting as well as timeless issues about war in general.

The 1978 film *Coming Home* is the story of a Vietnam veteran whose war injuries have turned him into a paraplegic, someone who is paralyzed below the waist. The film deals with the difficulties he faces in adjusting to life at home. That same year, two other movies raised questions about the effects of war. *The Deer Hunter* told the story of a disillusioned veteran returning from the Vietnam War, and *Who'll Stop the Rain* focused on soldiers who were drug runners while in Vietnam.

Antiwar Films

One of the most powerful of the antiwar films from the Vietnam War era was *Apocalypse Now*. This 1979 movie, based on the Joseph Conrad book *Heart of Darkness*, deals with the madness of war and how it changes and destroys human beings. Despite its controversial subject, *Apocalypse Now* was an immediate popular success. A week after the movie's release, it was packing in crowds. In the first six days of its run in only three theaters, the movie earned $385,000. Its popularity was a sign of the effect this

The theme of the Australian film Gallipoli *(1981) is of the disarray that war can bring.*

Apocalypse Now *(1979)* *depicts the madness of war* *and how it changes people* *from good to bad. The* *movie is based on Joseph* *Conrad's book* Heart of Darkness.

film would have on the nation.

Many soldiers who had served in Vietnam returned to the United States to find themselves the targets of anger by those who opposed the war. Some had deep psychological scars. Partly because the public wanted to forget the war, many of these soldiers were unable to discuss their experiences. *Apocalypse Now* helped change the public mood. The movie reminded the nation that the soldiers were not the cause of the war and that they too had suffered. In this way, the film helped create an atmosphere in which veterans could discuss their experiences in Vietnam with a nation now willing to listen.

American filmmakers were not the only ones making movies that questioned the actions, issues, and results of war. Some of these foreign films, often set during wars in the distant past, examined questions that remain relevant even today. The 1980 Australian film *Breaker Morant* was set during the turn-of-the-century Boer War in what is now South Africa. The movie raised the issue of how much responsibility an individual soldier has for his or her actions even when following orders. Another Australian movie, *Gallipoli,* made in 1981, focused on the destruction of war and the disarray that can result in the pointless death of soldiers.

Whether it is to gain support for a nation's troops or to question the reasons for war, movies have a tremendous power to mold public opinion. This power to influence has also shown itself in other ways by shaping people's ideas about their society and culture.

Race, Censorship, and Ratings

In both wartime and peacetime, movies have often been at the center of moral, religious, cultural, and political controversy. Sometimes, they are intended to be controversial, sometimes not. Whichever the case, movies have shattered social barriers and destroyed stereotypes. But they have also helped pass on prejudices from one generation to the next. Movies have helped shape standards of acceptable behavior, challenged moral values, and refuted as well as reinforced traditional notions of right and wrong. They have been the target of political

oppression as well as a tool used for achieving political change. For good or bad, movies have remained an influential force in society.

Stirring Hate

Since the first releases, motion pictures have helped spread prejudice and hate. Their targets were mainly blacks, Native American Indians, and other nonwhite cultural groups. The negative messages were picked up by thousands of Euro-

Actor Paul Newman starred in an updated version of Thomas Edison's original Buffalo Bill Cody's Wild West Show *(1976).*

The Ku Klux Klan, shown here at a modern rally, was portrayed favorably in D.W. Griffith's movie Birth of a Nation *(1915). The film ends with blacks being deported to Africa.*

pean immigrants pouring into the United States, seeking freedom and fortune. These immigrants desperately wanted to learn the ways of their new homeland, and movies seemed to offer a quick study in American values and customs.

For both the new arrivals and the established residents, "motion picture entertainment provided escapism and a sense of heightened self-esteem, particularly when white heroes could be seen besting members of other racial groups that were even lower on the socioeconomic scale," said Clint C. Wilson II, an associate dean at Howard University in Washington, D.C.

Indians Portrayed

Studios found that these types of movies were popular and profitable as early as 1898 when Edison filmed *Buffalo Bill Cody's Wild West Show.* In the show, Indians were portrayed as bloodthirsty and stupid. White cowboys and cowgirls were easily able to outride, outshoot, and outthink the movie Indians. Edison's film was incredibly popular, and

Birth of a Nation *is the story of a wealthy Southern family who loses everything during the Civil War. The villains, who are all black, are portrayed as savage, ignorant, lazy, and cruel.*

Millions of people have seen Birth of a Nation, *directed by D.W. Griffith, pictured here.*

film ever produced. Its director, D.W. Griffith, used every camera trick available and coupled these effects with a huge cast and famous stars to make it a film that everyone wanted to see. It quickly became the most popular movie of the era and audiences flocked to see it. What they saw was a film about a wealthy Southern family that loses everything during the Civil War. After the war, the family suffers at the hands of villains who take control of the South. The villains are all black. They are portrayed as savage, ignorant, lazy, and cruel. The family is ultimately saved by the Ku Klux Klan (KKK), a group that believes white people are superior to other races and uses violence to promote that belief. The film ends with its black characters being deported to Africa.

Millions saw Griffith's film. Many

with its success, the stereotypical movie Indian was born. For the next seventy years, films portrayed Indians as murderers, drunks, liars, and villains. Much of the American public came to believe that all Native Americans were like those shown in films. These beliefs helped promote discrimination against and hatred of Indians.

Servants and Clowns

Films have also shaped public attitudes about black Americans. In the earliest films, black characters were often portrayed as stupid, lazy, and corrupt. For the most part, the only roles for black actors were those of servants or bums whose clowning and stupidity were mocked throughout the film.

Among the most famous of these films was *Birth of a Nation*, made in 1915. At the time of its release, *Birth of a Nation* was the most technically dazzling

Actor Sidney Poitier portrays a northern black lawman in In the Heat of the Night *(1967). Actor Rod Steiger plays a white southern sheriff.*

In this scene from Guess Who's Coming to Dinner? *(1967), Sidney Poitier, Spencer Tracy, and Katharine Hepburn ponder the issue of interracial marriage.*

found no problem with his racist depictions of blacks and his implied message that black people should have been banished from the United States or remained chained in slavery. Some grade-school students were even taken to screenings of the film as part of their history lessons. Membership in the KKK swelled in the South, and new groups formed in the North. But the film also sparked anger and protest. The National Association for the Advancement of Colored People (NAACP) called for a boycott of the movie, asking people to refuse to see the movie as a way of protest. In Boston, five thousand people marched on the state capitol, demanding that the film be banned. When it was shown in Philadelphia, three thousand people rioted.

Breaking Barriers

Although some films have promoted stereotypes and hatred, others have broken racial and cultural barriers. More than other media, perhaps, motion pictures have built lifelike and engrossing stories around interesting people placed in all sorts of situations. They have exposed millions of viewers to different perspectives and new ideas and have done it in entertaining ways.

For these reasons, movies were able to examine issues that traditionally caused discomfort in the general public. In the 1960s, a time of great change in American society, movies dealt powerfully with two such issues. The 1967 film *In the Heat of the Night* tells the story of a racist white southern sheriff forced to work with a northern black lawman. Over the course of the film, it becomes apparent that the northerner, played by black actor Sidney Poitier, is much better at his job than the southern sheriff, played by white actor Rod Steiger. Steiger's character leaves no doubt about his negative feelings toward blacks. The movie audience gradually sees, however, that these views are based on ignorance. A second film, also released in 1967, addresses the emotional subject of interracial marriage. Many people have had difficulty—then and now—accepting the idea of marriage between people of different races. In the film *Guess Who's Coming to Dinner?*, a black man and white woman are engaged to marry. The marriage between the characters, played by Poitier and Katharine Houghton, challenged the notion that two people of different races could not marry and live a life like other married couples. As controversial as these films were, both drew huge crowds. *Guess Who's Coming to Dinner?* was, in fact, the second highest grossing film of the year.

Stereotypical views of Native Americans, many of which had been fueled by movies, have also been challenged by a few filmmakers. The 1970 film *Little Big Man* was one of the first to portray Indians as people with human values rather than as savage but futile warriors. More recently, the 1990 film *Dances With Wolves* portrays Native American Indians as people who, like others, experience hope, anger, desire, and fear.

Censorship

The movies' power to shape values and beliefs has always concerned some people, who periodically call for censorship. Some forms of censorship are as

Dances with Wolves (1990), starring Kevin Costner (right), illustrates the inhumane way American Indians were treated by white soldiers.

simple as using scissors to cut scenes considered objectionable. This type of censorship was common during the movie industry's early days. Most states hired people to preview films before they were released to the public. Their job was to cut inappropriate material. This was not always an easy task, mostly because ideas of what was objectionable differed from region to region. Women could be shown smoking on the screen in Ohio but not in Kansas. Pregnancy could be mentioned in movies shown in New York but not in Pennsylvania. In New York, censors objected to crime on the big screen. In one year alone, New York censors cut 3,005 violent crime scenes from films. In the Deep South, censors demanded the cutting of scenes that showed black people in any role other than servants.

Former postmaster general Will H. Hays (above) was hired to ensure that filmmakers did not violate the voluntary Production Code, which outlawed forbidden film topics.

As films passed from state to state, they were often edited in one state and then reedited in another. Sometimes censors cut so many scenes from a movie that it no longer made sense. One censor admitted that his censorship board had cut so many scenes from one film that on final viewing, "we had to stop in the middle of it, because we thought we were looking at the wrong [movie]."

Forbidden Topics

In an effort to save itself from this type of censorship, the movie industry formed the Motion Picture Producers and Distributors Association (MPPDA). This organization developed a list of forbidden topics and hired former postmaster general Will H. Hays to make sure filmmakers did not violate the new voluntary Production Code, as it was called. Forbidden topics under the code included various forms of sexuality, crime,

Little Big Man *(1970), starring Dustin Hoffman (above), broke new ground by portraying American Indians as people, rather than brutal, ruthless savages.*

In this 1951 photograph, actor John Garfield testifies before the House of Representatives Committee on Un-American Activities.

and drug abuse. Hays kept careful watch over movie content for many years. But even his scrutiny could not compare to a more subtle form of censorship imposed by the U.S. Congress.

Political Pressure

Congressional censorship took the form of political pressure and intimidation. And it worked, perhaps better than anything tried before. Beginning in the late 1940s, filmmakers avoided more subjects than ever, especially in the area of politics. Some projects were abandoned altogether, although their controversial nature was questionable. One such project was the film *Hiawatha,*

based on a poem by Henry Wadsworth Longfellow. In Longfellow's poem, the Indian chief Hiawatha urges warring Indian tribes to settle their differences peacefully. Fearing this would be viewed as somehow urging Americans to cease their fight against communism, the film's producers abandoned the project before it was completed.

All of this occurred during a time of mounting tension and mistrust between the world's two superpowers—the United States and Soviet Union. Any American appearing to sympathize or agree with Soviet ideologies was suspect. In this atmosphere, the House of Representatives Committee on Un-American Activities (HUAC) began a series of hearings in September 1947. Through these hearings, committee members hoped to send a message to the American public. They wanted all Americans to know that communism—the Soviet economic and political system in which private property is forbidden and the government controls production and distribution of all goods—would not be tolerated in the United States.

Communist Sympathizers

The motion picture industry was one of many targets of the investigating committee. But because it was a wealthy and influential industry, it was a particularly effective target to hit. The public would be sure to take notice of what happened. Between 1947 and 1951, the committee called on hundreds of movie people to testify. Many of those called were assumed to be Communist sympathizers, and committee members wanted them to expose others who might have Communist ties. Anyone suspected of having such ties, whether they actually did or not, was barred from working. This forced many people in the industry out of the business. By the time the hearings ended, the studios had fired 324 people. Many of these people were unable to find work in the American film industry. These included screenwriter Ring Lardner, Jr., whose screenplay for a film called *Woman of the Year* had won him an Academy Award just a few years earlier. Actor Howard Da Silva, who had played a kindly police chief in the 1951 movie *Fourteen Hours,* was also unable to find work. Actors John Garfield, who played an unprincipled prizefighter in the movie *The Life of Jimmy Dolan*; Edward Bromberg, who played a greedy governor in the 1940

movie *The Mark of Zorro*; and Mady Christians, who played the vicious aunt in the 1932 version of *Heidi,* all died soon after testifying before the committee. Their deaths were hastened, some said, by the stress of testifying. Other people in the industry left the country to look for work.

The HUAC investigation affected the kinds of movies produced for close to fifteen years. From the beginning of the investigation until the beginning of the socially conscious 1960s, Hollywood stayed away from controversial films. Historically, movies had been used to discuss issues people found difficult to talk about. Motion pictures brought these issues into the open for debate. But political intimidation helped silence the movies, and Hollywood instead tried to make films designed simply to entertain. But even these films raised objections from people who thought moviemakers were using too much sex and violence to hold the public's attention.

Sex and Violence

With the increase in the amount of movie sex and violence came the debate of how much is too much. People began to worry about what would happen if audiences continued to watch movies filled with sex and violence. Moviegoers were able to see things on the screen that had never been discussed in public before. Films depicting promiscuity and criminal behavior seemed to be challenging the country's traditional beliefs in modesty, chastity, and lawful actions.

The concern over the impact of sex and violence on viewers has existed

Other Men's Women *(1931) seemed to promote extramarital affairs. This enraged some people.*

since the era of silent films. People have always worried that watching films would inspire viewers to copy what they saw on the screen. In 1907, the *Chicago*

Tribune wrote that "[movies are] without [any] redeeming feature to warrant their existence. . . . [It is] proper to suppress them at once." The same year, a censorship board was established in Chicago to edit films and shield people whose "age, education and situation entitle them to protection against the evil influence" of the movies. The first silent movie banned was a film version of Shakespeare's *Macbeth*. The board thought a stabbing scene in the film was too violent. Censors were concerned that someone watching the scene might try to imitate it.

Copy the Actors

Concern about films continued to grow as talking movies developed. Once film actors began to speak, the movies seemed more realistic. And, as many people feared, the public began to copy the actions they saw on movie screens. Grade-school children started smoking

The Strange Love of Molly Louvain *(1932) portrayed women having sexual affairs with many partners. This and other films of its era seemed to violate the morals of most families.*

Parents and religious leaders were enraged by movies like Blonde Crazy *(1931), which featured women indulging in drunken sprees and sexual escapades.*

cigarettes and imitating the tough talk of gangsters after seeing such movies as *Public Enemy*, made in 1931, and *Scarface*, made in 1932. The heroes of these films lied, cheated, robbed, and killed, and some parents worried that their children would also follow these examples. A book released in 1933 titled *Our Movie-Made Children* argued that these types of films were corrupting children and making them juvenile delinquents.

Parents and religious leaders were also enraged by the amount of sex in films. Movies like *Other Men's Women* made in 1931 seemed to promote extramarital affairs. *Blonde Crazy* made in 1931 and *The Strange Love of Molly Louvain* made in 1932 featured women who went from sexual partner to partner. These movies told the stories of women who indulged in drunken sprees and sexual escapades. Films like these seemed to promote ideas that violated the morals of most families.

A Call for Clean Movies

In response to these depictions of sex and "sin" in movies, the Roman Catholic Church formed the Legion of Decency in December 1933. The group called for people to boycott immoral films. Ten million Americans joined the legion. They pledged to "remain away from all motion pictures except those which do not offend decency and Christian morality." In addition to boycotting movies, the legion began lobbying Congress to pass censorship laws.

Can Can *(1960) was one of the first movies to openly violate the Production Code.*

In an effort to appease the Legion of Decency, members of the MPPDA voted to make the Production Code mandatory. Filmmakers agreed to submit their movies to the MPPDA for approval. Theater owners agreed not to show films unless they carried the MPPDA seal of approval. The MPPDA also voted to levy a fine of twenty-five thousand dollars against members who released a movie without the seal.

Controversial Issues

The Production Code stopped most of the complaints from people who wanted to censor films. But it also stopped studios from making many movies that dealt with real-life prob-

lems. After the code became mandatory, filmmakers no longer discussed the problems of crime, alcoholism, or any issues dealing with sex. Once again, films lost their ability to speak out on controversial social issues.

This type of self-censorship continued until the 1960s, when audiences began to demand more realistic films. European films, many of which dealt with adult themes of sex and violence, were being shown in American theaters. Independent producers were making films forbidden by the code and showing them in small theaters that were not part of the MPPDA. These films were financially very successful, and the public demanded more. At the same time, the American public was becoming more liberal. These were the days of hippies and the sexual revolution. What shocked 1940s audiences seemed conservative in the 1960s. Hollywood began to crank out films that violated the Production Code.

One of the first was the 1960 film *Can Can,* which tells the story of a young judge who indulges in drunken sprees and nights of vice with women of ill repute. This movie was overshadowed by the 1962 version of Hemingway's novel *The Sun Also Rises,* which is filled with characters who travel from party to party and lover to lover. Studios also rediscovered violence. In 1967, *The St. Valentine's Day Massacre* re-created the era in which gangsters Al Capone and Bugsy Moran lived and showed onscreen an abundance of machine guns and bloodshed. In 1968, audiences were treated to graphic descriptions of bodies being dismembered in *The Detective.*

Death of the Code

With so many studios violating the code, it virtually lost all of its power. On November 1, 1968, the Production Code was abolished and replaced by a new rating system. The rating system was designed to allow moviemakers to produce films with adult themes and to allow audiences to choose the type of film they wanted to see. Ratings were divided into four categories: G for general audiences; M for mature audiences; R for audiences over age eighteen; and X for audiences over twenty-one. Throughout the years, the rating system has changed slightly. The classification of R was changed to allow admittance of children under seventeen as long as they were accompanied by an adult; the X

rating was lowered to age seventeen; and the M was replaced with PG, which stands for "parental guidance suggested." In 1984, a new rating of PG-13 was added to designate films requiring special guidance for children under thirteen. The last change to the system came in 1990, when the X rating was dropped and replaced with NC-17, which means no children under seventeen admitted. The rating was changed because the X rating had become synonymous with pornography, or material that depicts erotic behavior intended to cause sexual excitement. As a result, many serious and artistic films were avoided by theaters and viewers who thought the movies would be pornographic.

Ratings are assigned by the Classifi-

Sex and violence were seen throughout The St. Valentine's Day Massacre *(1967). The movie re-created the gangster era of Al Capone and Bugsy Moran.*

cation and Ratings Administration (CARA) board of the Motion Picture Association of America (MPAA). The board is made up of ten Los Angeles-area parents selected by the board's chairman, Richard Heffner. Board members come from a variety of backgrounds. They are laborers, schoolteachers, executives, and homemakers. Being a parent is the only requirement for being on the board. The board convenes five days a week at the MPAA office in Sherman Oaks, California, to screen films and assign ratings.

New Type of Censorship?

The rating system was designed to give filmmakers more freedom. But for many, the rating system seemed to be a new type of censorship. Once again, filmmakers found themselves cutting films and avoiding certain subject matter to keep from receiving an X or NC-17 rating. Usually an "adults only" rat-

ing means the ruin of a film. Most theaters that belong to the MPAA refuse to show an X or NC-17 film out of fear of being associated with pornographic films. A theater's refusal to show a film means the loss of thousands of dollars of profit for filmmakers. Also, most newspapers refuse to carry advertising for films with X ratings. This often means that even if a studio can find a theater to show its film, there is still the problem of not being able to advertise where the film is playing.

Because of this situation, most filmmakers try to edit their movies to receive an R rating. Others are unwilling to edit and say the ratings board is too arbitrary and unfair. Some critics contend that artistic films are often rated NC-17 simply because board members are uncomfortable with the subject, even though they grant mainstream movies with more sex and violence an R rating. One example is the 1990 film *Henry and June,* the first film to receive an NC-17 rating. Critics of the ratings

Henry and June (1990) was the first movie to receive an NC-17 rating. This rating dictates that no one under seventeen is allowed to view it.

Some people say Taxi Driver *(1976) has stirred people to violence. John Hinckley, Jr., said he got the idea to shoot President Ronald Reagan after watching the movie.*

pealing to a twenty-two member MPAA appeals board made up of theater owners. In order to overturn a rating, two-thirds of the appeals board must agree to reverse the earlier decision. But the appeals process can be lengthy, and the board usually supports the initial rating. In twenty-two years, only 228 appeals have been filed, and only 101 of these rulings have been overturned. Instead of appealing, many moviemakers either edit films to keep them within the R rating or avoid making films dealing with objectionable topics.

Lingering Questions

Even with moviemakers willing to cut controversial scenes, movies are still filled with sex and violence. And many people still worry about how much is too much. Concerned groups cite *The Deer Hunter* (1978) and *Taxi Driver* (1976) as examples of movies that stir people to violence. Twenty-eight people allegedly died playing Russian roulette, a game of chance using a loaded gun, after seeing the game in *The Deer Hunter*. And John Hinckley, Jr., said he developed the idea of shooting President Ronald Reagan after watching *Taxi Driver*. Because of these cases, many people still think movies should be censored to protect the public. These are issues that will follow the industry into the future.

board say this film received an adults-only rating simply because it dealt with female homosexuality.

If the board gives an NC-17 rating to a film, producers have the option of ap-

CHAPTER 8

Into the Future

In the future, people will no longer simply watch films but will experience them. Instead of being windows to other worlds, movies will be doors to walk through. In the future, audiences will no longer be passive viewers but active participants in films.

Ride a Magic Carpet

The move from simply watching a film to experiencing it started in 1990 when Imax Systems Corporation began test-

With specially designed gloves, a virtual reality participant could manipulate objects that exist in the movie.

ing the Magic Carpet System. When the system is perfected, perhaps within the next five years, it will allow audiences to feel as if they are riding a magic carpet through a movie instead of viewing it on a screen.

To enhance the reality of a film, viewers will be totally surrounded by images. In the Magic Carpet System, the main viewing screen will be seven stories tall. In addition, there will be screens on the sides, ceiling, and floor of the theater. These screens will help immerse the audience in the movie. If a film includes a flight scene, for example, clouds will be projected above, below, and around the audience. Surrounded by these visions, viewers should experience the feeling of floating through the sky. In an ocean sequence, audiences will be able to experience the feeling of living underwater. Sharks will swim by viewers, and schools of fish will dart above them.

Touching New Worlds

While scientists work to perfect the Magic Carpet System, other researchers are working to take audiences one step farther. When perfected, computer-generated virtual reality will create new worlds that audiences can reach out and touch. A number of U.S. and foreign companies are working on the concept.

To enter virtual reality, the participant wears specially designed gloves

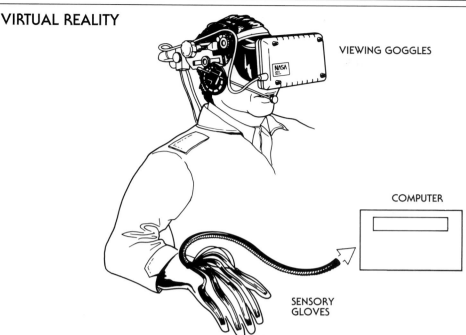

VIRTUAL REALITY

VIEWING GOGGLES

COMPUTER

SENSORY
GLOVES

Movie producers are now working on virtual reality, a computer-simulated experience that so closely imitates real life that the "virtual" experience is scarcely distinguishable from the real one.

To experience virtual reality, the moviegoer wears specially designed gloves and goggles that are linked to sophisticated computers. The goggles contain a video screen for each eye. If a movie contains a scene of a mountain, for example, the viewer could reach out to touch it, and stand up and move his feet in place to climb it. Sensors on the moviegoer's hands would give him the sensation of touching the rough, craggy surface of the mountain. The computer would continually update the images in the goggles so the viewer would have the feeling that he was climbing higher and higher.

At the same time, the special gloves allow the viewer to manipulate objects that exist in the movie. So, if the viewer wanted to reach down and pick a flower, for example, the gloves would supply the sensation of touching the flower, even though the viewer would be touching nothing at all.

and goggles linked to a sophisticated computer. The goggles contain two video screens, one for each eye. The screens show three-dimensional scenes that seem to totally surround the wearer. Instead of sitting passively, viewers leave their chairs and walk through movie scenes. Every time a viewer moves his head or hands, electronic sensors inside the goggles and gloves send signals to the computer. The computer then changes the images on the video screens to match the viewer's new position.

If a film contained a shot of a house, for example, the viewer could actually take a walking tour of the entire house. Following the movements of the goggles and gloves, the computer would be able to present an accurate image of the house. With the help of the sensors and computer, the viewer could walk down corridors, peer around corners, or glance over a shoulder to see if anyone is following.

The wearer would experience the feeling of touching and picking up things in the film. Using the special gloves, viewers could open doors or pick up books from a shelf. A pressing sensation supplied by the gloves would give the wearer a real sense of feeling something, even though the wearer would be touching nothing.

Is It Live or Just a Computer Image?

The advanced computers used to create virtual reality will also change the way films are made. Once a film is shot, directors will use computers to change or edit scenery and props.

Computer editing will also allow filmmakers to erase actors from a film and replace them with new performers or computer images. The computer images would be so lifelike that no one would be able to tell the difference between the images and the human actors. Once the technology is in place, perhaps early in the next century, filmmakers could produce entire movies without a single human being, according to Bob Schneider, a professor of video and film at Southwestern College in Chula Vista, California.

In the past, movies were made with images captured on film. In the future, computers may eliminate the need for film altogether, Schneider said. "As we move into computers, which generate images on their own, we may move away from photographs. It would even be possible to create a feature film that is populated with human characters that are not human but are all completely computer-generated. If you create computer characters, you can have them do things that humans can't do," Schneider said. Computer characters could easily fly, or change shape, or do whatever a director required, stunts that

Computer-generated virtual reality may someday allow moviegoers to experience new worlds. To enter virtual reality, a participant wears goggles that contain video screens. A sophisticated computer changes the images on the screens according to the participant's action.

The computer may someday be able to pair modern-day stars such as Mel Gibson with deceased stars to create new and exciting movies.

fected, moviegoers may be able to custom-design the movies they watch. Such films, called interactive films, would allow viewers to choose actions for the screen heroes. For example, in a science-fiction thriller, a viewer could decide if the hero fights an alien or flees simply by pushing a button. The viewer's choice would determine the next scene in the film. This interactive feature would give a single film hundreds of possible story lines.

Interactive films may also be linked with virtual reality to make the computer-generated worlds more realistic. Researchers at Carnegie-Mellon University in Pittsburgh, Pennsylvania, are already working on combining the two technologies. Researchers hope to make computer-generated characters who can adapt to the actions of the audience. But the end result of this research is years in the future.

now can be performed only with the help of expensive special effects.

In addition to creating new characters, the computer could bring dead actors back to life. Images of anyone who has ever appeared on film could be fed into the computer and re-created. This means 1950s movie sex symbol Marilyn Monroe, who died in 1962, could star with modern-day heartthrob Mel Gibson in a new movie. Winston Churchill, who died in 1965, could be re-created to star in a movie about World War II. The possibilities would be limited only by the director's imagination.

As the computer film systems are per-

Movie Magic

The more realistic films become, the more magical they will seem. Since motion pictures made their debut at the turn of the century, they have captivated audiences. Current innovations promise that movies will not lose their power to enthrall audiences. As new technology replaces old filmmaking techniques, the movies will take us to places that we can now reach only in our imagination.

Glossary

celluloid: A substance used to record photographs. It was similar to modern film but was very stiff.

exposure: Allowing light to strike the surface of the film.

film: A strong, transparent, and flexible material covered with a light-sensitive coating so that photographs can be recorded on it.

frame: An individual picture on a length of film.

Kinetograph: The first true motion picture camera.

live action: The real movements of people or things as opposed to animation.

magic lantern: An ordinary rectangular box with a round hole cut in one side used to project images in a darkened room.

narrative film: A movie that tells a story and has a beginning, middle, and end.

nickleodeon: The first permanent movie theater.

panorama: A large painting that gives a comprehensive picture of a chain of events.

persistence of vision: The phenomenon in which an image remains on the retina of the eye for a fraction of a second after the image disappears from sight, causing the eye to perceive movement if a succession of still pictures is changed rapidly.

rating: A system of film classification based on the amount of violence, sex, or controversial language in a movie.

reel: Film on a spool for use in projectors.

shutter: The mechanism that opens and closes the opening that allows light into the camera to expose the film.

sprocket holes: Punched-out holes near the edge of the film used to hold the film securely in the camera.

stop action: A trick photography technique that makes it possible for objects to appear and disappear by exposing frames of film one at a time and by moving the objects being filmed between frames.

superimpose: To combine two images, one on top of the other, on one piece of film by running the film through the camera twice.

For Further Reading

Don Allen, *The World of Film and Filmmakers*. New York: Crown, 1979.

Joel Finler, *The Hollywood Story*. New York: Crown, 1988.

Ralph and Natasha A. Friar, *The Only Good Indian . . . The Hollywood Gospel*. New York: Drama Book Specialists/Publishers, 1972.

Brock Garland, *War Movies*. New York: Facts on File Publications, 1987.

Harry Geduld, *The Birth of the Talkies*. Bloomington: Indiana University Press, 1975.

Barry Norman, *The Story of Hollywood*. New York: NAL Books, 1987.

Works Consulted

■ ■

Maurice Bardeche, *History of the Motion Pictures.* New York: Norton, 1938.

Jeanne Bendick, *Making The Movies.* New York: McGraw-Hill, 1945.

Terry Christensen, *Reel Politics.* New York: Basil Blackwell, 1987.

David Cook, *A History of Narrative Film.* New York: Norton, 1981.

Jack Ellis, *A History of Film.* Englewood Cliffs, NJ: Prentice-Hall, 1979.

George MacDonald Fraser, *The Hollywood History of the World.* New York: Beech Tree Books, 1988.

A. R. Fulton, *Motion Pictures—The Development of an Art.* Norman: University of Oklahoma Press, 1960.

James Hurt, *Focus on Film and Theater.* Englewood Cliffs, NJ: Prentice-Hall, 1974.

James Limbacher, *Four Aspects of the Film.* New York: Brussel & Brussel, 1968.

James Monaco, "Into the '90s," *American Film,* Jan/Feb 1989.

Victor Navasky, *Naming Names.* New York: Viking, 1980.

Popular Photography, "Floating in Space," July 1990.

George Pratt, *Spellbound in Darkness—A History of the Silent Film.* New York: Graphic Society, 1973.

Martin Quigley, Jr., *Magic Shadows—The Story of the Origin of Motion Pictures.* Washington, D.C.: Georgetown University Press, 1948.

David Robinson, *The History of World Cinema.* New York: Stein & Day, 1973.

Dennis Sharp, *The Picture Palace.* New York: Frederick, 1969.

Robert Vaughn, *Only Victims.* New York: Putnam's, 1972.

David Manning White and Richard Averson, *The Celluloid Weapon, Social Comment in the American Film.* Boston: Beacon Press, 1972.

Index

■ ■

actors
  fashion trends and, 39, 49
  role in wars, 59-60, 63-64
  silent films and, 35-39, 45-48
  sound films and, 45-48, 51-52
  star system, development of, 37-39
  studios
    contracts with, 51-52
    working conditions, 52-53
All Quiet on the Western Front, 67
Apocalypse Now, 68-69
Armat, Thomas, 28

Barker, Robert, 12
Birth of a Nation, 35, 40, 72-73
Blackton, J. Stuart, 59

Casler, Hermann, 28
Celluloid, 22
Chaplin, Charlie, 37-38
Childe, Henry Langdon, 15-16
Churchill, Winston, 64
Coleman, Ronald, 48
Confessions of a Nazi Spy, 61-62
Creel, George, 60

Daguerre, Louis Jacques Mande, 12-13
De Forest, Lee, 41-42
Dickson, William Laurie Kennedy, 24, 28, 40

Eastman, George, 22-23
Edison, Thomas, 28, 29, 33
  inventor of
    Kinetograph, 23-24
    Kinetophone, 40-41
    Kinetoscope, 23-26

film
  Celluloid, 22
  development of, 22-23
  Photographic Pellicle, 22

Garbo, Greta, 47-48, 49
Goldstein, Robert, 60
Goodwin, Hannibal Williston, 22
Great Train Robbery, The, 32-33
Griffith, D.W., 34-36, 72

Hays, Will H., 75-76
Heffner, Richard, 82
Henry V, 64
Hitler, Adolf, 65
Hollywood
  history, 34
Horner, William George, 16
Hyatt, John Wesley, 22

Ince, Thomas, 50-51

Janssen, Pierre Jules, 19-20
Jazz Singer, The, 43-44
Jolson, Al, 43-44

Kaufman, Joe, 62

Laemmle, Carl, 38
Latham, Gray, 29
Latham, Otway, 29
Lawrence, Florence, 38
limelights, 15
Lumiere, Auguste and Louis
  inventors of Cinematographe, 26
    first public showing, 27
    populairty of, 27-28, 30

Marey, Etienne-Jules, 19-21
Marvin, Henry, 28
Melies, George, 30-32
Metro-Goldwyn-Mayer (MGM), 51
Miranda, Carmen, 49
movie cameras and projectors
  futuristic
    computer editing, 85-86

interactive films, 86-87
Magic Carpet System, 84
three-dimensional (3-D), 85
virtual reality, 84-87
history
Cinematographe, 26-28
dioramas, 12-13
Kinetograph, 23-24
Kinetophone, 40-41
Kinetoscope, 23-25, 40-41
  copies, 25-26
limelights, 15
magic lanterns, 13-15
Mutoscope, 28
panoramic murals, 12
peepshows, 25
Phantasmagoria, 15
photography and, 18-21
photo revolver, 19-21
Praxinoscope, 17-18
sound, 40-42
Vitaphone, 41-42
Vitascope, 29
Zoetrope, 16-17
Zoopraxiscope, 19
persistence of Vision, 16-17
movies
censorship
cutting scenes, 74-75
House Un-American Activities Committee
  (HUAC), 76-77
Legion of Decency, 79-80
Motion Picture Association of America
  (MPAA), 82
Motion Picture Producers and Distributors
  Association (MPPDA), 75, 80
political, 76-77
Production Code, 75, 80
ratings, 81-83
sex and violence, 77-81, 83
slapstick comedy, 36-38

war, 61
competition against
radio, 42-43
television, 54-57
history
animal movement, 19
Biograph, 28
color, 56-57
editing, 32-33
first public showings, 26-28, 29, 31
Great Train Robbery, The, 32-33
Jazz Singer, The, 43-44
Keystone Studios, 36
Motion Pictures Patents Company
  (MPPC), 34
photography in, 18-21
silent films, 35, 42
sound, 40-44
Star Film Company, 31
Technicolor, 56
trick photography, 30-31
Warner Brothers, 43
racism in
American Indians, 71-72, 74
Birth of a Nation, 72-73
black Americans, 72-74
interracial marriage, 73-74
Ku Klux Klan (KKK), 72-73
studios
actors contracts with, 51-52
system, development of, 50-51
theaters, ownership of, 53-54
three-dimensional (3-D) films, 54-56, 85
war and
All Quiet on the Western Front, 67
antiwar films, 67-69
Apocalypse Now, 68-69
censorship, 61
Committee on Public Information (CPI),
  60
Confessions of a Nazi Spy, 61-62

Germany, 60, 65-66
Great Britain, 63-65
Henry V, 64
Mexico, 58-59
propaganda, 59, 60, 62-66
semidocumentaries, 64-65
Spanish-American War, 59
Vietnam, 68-69
War Activities Committee, 63
World War I, 59-60
World War II, 60-66
Muybridge, Eadweard, 18-19

nickelodeons, 33

Olivier, Laurence, 64

Paul, Robert, 25-26
persistence of vision, 16-17
Photographic Pellicle, 22
photography
  film speed, 18
  history of movies and, 18-21
Porter, Edwin S., 32
propaganda, 59, 60, 63-66

Reynaud, Emile, 17-18
Robertson, Etienne Gaspard, 15
Roosevelt, Theodore, 59

Schneider, Bob, 86
Sennett, Mack, 36

Talbot, Henry Fox, 18
theaters
  history
    movie studio ownership, 53-54
    nickelodeons, 33
three-dimensional (3-D) films, 54-56, 85

Valentino, Rudolph, 39

Villa, Pancho, 58-59
virtual reality, 84-87

Warner Brothers, 43-44, 51, 61-62
Wilson, Clint C., 71

About the Authors

Deborah Hitzeroth currently lives in California, where she is working on her M.A. degree in English. Her writing background includes a B.A. degree in journalism from the University of Missouri and four years of newspaper experience. Following a brief stint as a section editor on a weekly paper, she worked as a free-lance writer for a monthly medical magazine in New York. Her hobbies include scuba diving, traveling, and the movies. This is her third book.

Sharon Heerboth currently lives in Texas. She has a B.S. degree from the University of Missouri and an A.A. degree from Texas State Technical Institute. Her writing background includes in-house technical and educational writing. Her hobbies include waterskiing, gardening, reading, and the movies. This is her first book.

Picture Credits

■■■

Photos supplied by Research Plus, Inc., Mill Valley, California

Cover photo by Photofest

American Stock/Pictorial Parade, 45, 52

AP/Wide World Photos, 51, 76

The Bettmann Archive, 15, 17, 20 (both), 30, 31, 32, 36, 38, 57, 75

Robert Coldwell, 16, 25, 27, 41, 55, 85

Hollywood Book and Poster, 35, 37, 39, 44, 45, 46, 53, 63, 65, 67 (both), 68, 69, 71, 74, 75, 80, 82, 83, 87

Frederick Lewis Stock Photos, 12, 13, 22, 23, 48

Memory Shop West, 34, 70, 73

The Museum of Modern Art, 18

The Museum of Modern Art/Film Stills Archive, 24

National Archives, 42, 62

Pictorial Parade, Inc., 23, 36, 47, 49, 51, 58, 61, 64, 66, 71, 72 (both), 78 (both), 79, 81

Pictorial Picture, Inc., 14

U.S. Department of Interior, National Park Service, Edison National Historic Site, 26, 27, 29

VPL Research, 84, 86